TURN OF THE CENTURY
American Dinnerware
1880s to 1920s

Joanne Jasper

COLLECTOR BOOKS

A Division of Schroeder Publishing Co., Inc.

The current values in this book should be used only as a guide. They are not intended to set prices, which vary from one section of the country to another. Auction prices as well as dealer prices vary greatly and are affected by condition as well as demand. Neither the Author nor the Publisher assumes responsibility for any losses that might be incurred as a result of consulting this guide.

Searching for a Publisher?

We are always looking for knowledgeable people considered to be experts within their fields. If you feel that there is a real need for a book on your collectible subject and have a large comprehensive collection, contact COLLECTOR BOOKS.

On the Cover:
Top Left:
Homer Laughlin "Hudson" Casserole, $35.00 – 45.00.
Top Right:
KTK "Nevada" 8 pr Jug, $55.00 – 65.00.
Bottom Right:
Argosy Sugar, $14.00 – 16.00.
Bottom Left:
KTK Commandery Plate, $45.00 – 65.00.
Center Left:
KTK "Traymore" Sugar, $14.00 – 16.00.
Center:
West End Pottery Advertising Plate, $20.00 – 30.00.

Cover design: Beth Summers
Book design: Michelle Dowling

Additional copies of this book may be ordered from:

COLLECTOR BOOKS
P.O. BOX 3009
Paducah, Kentucky 42002–3009
or
Joanne Jasper
28005 Balkins Drive
Agoura Hills, CA 91301

@ $24.95. Add $2.00 for postage and handling.

Contents

Introduction

While I was writing my first book, on Homer Laughlin decorated china, I often encountered pieces of old china which at first I thought were from HLC. However, when I turned these over to look at the marks, I discovered they were from other, lesser-known American potteries. During my research efforts on the first book, I learned of the extensive and prosperous china-making industry in America, back around the turn of the century. This industry was concentrated in places like Trenton, New Jersey, and East Liverpool, Ohio. While there were a few potters who continued operation over lengthy periods, many were active for only a few years. Nevertheless, the handiwork of these bygone industries is often found in antiques shops today.

Wares made by these old potteries are often seen in antiques stores, but information about the china and potters themselves is in much shorter supply. Perhaps I was spoiled by Homer Laughlin, which not only marked their wares with stamps that could easily be dated, but more importantly, had remained in operation for over 100 years. Their extensive records, augmented by the personal memories of the management and employees, have made the research and documentation of their history a breeze. Contrast this with the others, who suffered from bankruptcies, fires, floods, not to mention both hostile and benign takeovers by competing firms. Records were destroyed by nature. What information survived these natural disasters was later subjected to the disinterest of people who simply threw the beautiful old catalogs and operating records away in the trash.

Although the historical record is sketchy, I have still been fortunate to have obtained access to many catalogs published by potters of the East Liverpool district, which are held in the archives of the East Liverpool Museum of Ceramics. The staff there has graciously allowed me to examine and photograph many of the documents. My quest for similar information about potters of the Trenton area has, unfortunately, not been so rewarding. Still, there are countless pages from extinct trade publications which can still shed light on the china-making efforts from this period. Finally, I have had an opportunity to contact historical archaeologists engaged in the excavation of the sites of turn-of-the-century buildings, in whose ruins have been found fragments of china from this same period. It has been exciting to handle these old shards, and to realize that on such-and-such a day that dish was in use at a particular hotel which had then burned to the ground.

While I have tried in these pages to revisit the history of the old potters and potteries, I have also attempted to emphasize information of a practical nature, for the use of dealers and collectors of this china. For these readers, the main questions I have tried to answer were: "What is it, where did it come from, what is it worth, and is there more out there like it?"

Acknowledgments

I owe a great deal to the people who supplied me with information, photographs, and dishes. Judi Wilfong of Buffalo, Texas, and Richard Racheter of St. Petersburg, Florida, who sent pictures of Homer Laughlin China from their very large collections, and in Richard's case, not only supplied pictures but wonderful write-ups which were a great help and are reflected in some places in this book. Bill and Donna Gray of Columbia, Maryland, welcomed me into their home and helped me photograph many lovely pieces from their large collection of old American dinnerware. Leota Bohnert of Charleston, West Virginia, found and mailed to me many of the china dishes seen photographed in these pages. Also thanks to the following people:

Darlene Nossaman	Waco, Texas
Lois Lehner	Radnor, Ohio
Harvey Duke	Brooklyn, New York
Bill Mackall, Tudordane Antiques	East Liverpool, Ohio
Steve Sfakis	East Liverpool, Ohio
Joan Witt	East Liverpool, Ohio
Ed Carson	East Liverpool, Ohio
Kathy of Penny Pinchers Antiques	Simi Valley, California
Frederick Morth	Rehoboth, Massachusetts
David J. Goldberg	Lawrenceville, New Jersey
Charles Webster	Trenton Public Library
Susan Finkel	New Jersey State Museum
Susan Walters	Chula Vista, California
Bryan Davis	Clovis, California
Kathy of Osterberg's Mercantile	Clovis, California
Lorna & Mick Chase, Fiesta Plus	Cooksville, Tennessee
Dick & Rosemarie Lewis	Columbia, Maryland
Chip Simpson & Jeanie Milburn	Baltimore, Maryland
Sandy Kalison	Bloomsburg, Pennsylvania
H. Frederick & Doris Whitney	Sebring, Ohio

My thanks to the people at the Westlake Photo Lab in Westlake Village, California, who did such a good job of making sure the dishes in the photos turned out in all their correct colors.

Donna Juszczak, Peggy Ferguson, and Dorrie Russell at the East Liverpool Museum of Ceramics were wonderful help. My thanks to them. If you get a chance to visit the Museum of Ceramics in East Liverpool, Ohio, it is well worth the extra trip.

Thanks again to the people at the Homer Laughlin China Company who so kindly gave me the run of the factory while doing my research: Dave Conley; J.M. Wells, Jr.; J.M. Wells, III; and especially Mr. Pete Aaron, II.

Also, again thanks to the Corning Museum of Glass in Corning, New York, for sending many, many reels of old microfilm.

While staying in the East Liverpool area I was given a roof over my head (and in fact treated like a queen) and driven around to pick up old dinnerware and check out current prices by my good friends Neva and Don Colbert. I love you.

As usual my greatest thanks must go to my husband, John, who is more than my editor, he co-authored many pages in this book. He kept the computer running despite everything I tried to do to it, and always had Anzio's pizza available as we worked our way to the end of the book.

Problems in Identifying Old China

When collectors encounter a piece of antique dinnerware, the first question usually asked is: "What is it called?" Antique dinnerware is identified by the name of the manufacturer, plus a name given to the particular form of all of the pieces making up a set (called the *shape* name), plus a name given to the colored decoration (called the *pattern* name). The name of the potter, the name of the shape, and the name of the pattern all influence the value of antique china. Pieces with no names are simply not as interesting to collectors.

For dinnerware made in the 1940s and after, shape and pattern names can be determined relatively easily. Shape names were given by manufacturers and in some cases by the larger mail-order houses. The retail sellers also provided their own pattern names, and when they didn't, the manufacturers often provided their own. These names can be found in the catalog pages which advertised the china, if not in the catalogs put out by the manufacturers themselves. The story is somewhat different for American dinnerware from around the turn of the century.

All potters (at least from the regions and time periods I have covered) seem to have proudly named all of the different shapes they produced. During the time period in question, manufacturers often announced new shapes or advertised them in any of several trade publications of the time. These announcements and advertisements often provide a picture of the ware, thereby associating the shape name and the appearance. In addition, the different potteries published catalogs which allow the appearance of a piece to be associated with its shape name. In most cases, shape names could be determined and have been provided in this book. However, for some potteries the printed records that have survived have not been sufficient to reveal the shape name given to a piece of china. In this case, I have just used the potter's name (obtained from the mark) together with a number I have assigned that will serve to identify both the shape *and* the decorative treatment. (Example: Anchor 100 — Anchor is the potter's name and 100 is the identifier of both the shape and decoration.)

Naming the decorations applied to the wares is a much more difficult process. In the first place, the taste for decoration during that time period tended more often to schemes in which the pattern was molded into the piece itself, rather than applied after the initial firing in the form of a decal. The molded decoration was then highlighted by painted-on colors or gold, but no one apparently thought to give a *name* to this colored treatment. Even in the cases where the pieces are decorated with a decal, the catalog will refer to it simply as "Rose and Lily of the Valley decoration," a descriptive but otherwise ordinary appellation. In short, there simply were no pattern names for most of the old dinnerware, not from the maker, and not from the seller. Accordingly, where I have been able to determine the name of the shape, but not the name of the decoration applied to the shape, I have given the decoration my own pattern number, appended to the name of the shape. (Example: Hudson 100 — Hudson is the shape name of a Homer Laughlin dinnerware and 100 is the identifier of the decoration.)

In my descriptions used in the value guide, I have attempted to minimize the sizing confusion by using volume in ounces or pints whenever referring to the size of a piece intended to contain fluids, if the information is available. Often the only way to get this information is to fill the piece with water, and then measure how much water it held. If this was not possible, and the volume is not otherwise known, the size will be in terms of inches or the number that will fit into a barrel.

Flatware measurements will be provided in inches. If the actual size is stated by the pottery, then I used this size. Otherwise, I just measured the piece with a tape measure and that is the dimension that is stated in the text.

The Anchor Pottery Company was located in the Trenton, New Jersey, potting region. Like other companies from that area, historical information about Anchor is difficult to come by. Anchor was founded by J.E. Norris in 1893. Early marks can be seen which contain his initials. After World War I, the company was acquired by the Grand Union Tea Company, which used Anchor to produce premiums which were given away in their house-to-house sales program. In 1926 Anchor was bought by the Fulper Pottery Company. To my knowledge, no wares are produced today which bear the Anchor mark.

I have been successful in locating several examples of serving pieces. Some were found on the West Coast, and some rather surprisingly in East Liverpool. I thought Anchor wares would have been easy to find in New Jersey, but a quick trip through literally dozens of antiques stores turned up not a single piece.

The Anchor wares that I have examined reveal a medium quality workmanship. The designs range from the simple to the extremely ornate, as shown by the examples in Plates 6 and 7. A final note about Anchor designs: an Anchor platter was found which appeared to be an exact copy of a Warwick platter, also in my collection. The two pieces are identical in every respect, down to the shape and the details of the embossing, although the surface decorations are much different. I have no idea why this is true. The marks on both pieces suggested they were made during the same period, so I cannot even speculate on who copied whom. This is another of the little curiosities that make antique china collecting so fascinating.

See value guide page 10.

Plate 1: Anchor back-stamp dated 1904 to 1912.

Plate 2: Anchor 100. White granite 10" plate with large yellow parrot decal.

Plate 3: Anchor 101. Cable-style teapot with blue and yellow parrot decal. This teapot and the 10" plate above are from the collection of Frederick Morth.

Plate 4: Anchor 102. This 15" platter with blue and pink flowers and heavy, gold covered embossing is identical to a platter made by Warwick. The backstamp is the only way they can be told apart.

Plate 5: Anchor 103. 13" dish (platter) and tureen, decorated with the pink and blue flowers which seem to have been a favorite of Anchor and many other American potteries of this period.

Description points to look for: The 15" platter has an irregular scalloped edge. The casserole has a very sturdy, scalloped foot which is impressed with a pattern of ridges and a finial that resembles a Chinese bridge.

Plate 6: Anchor 103. Sauce boat, with a large decal of a pheasant, clearly is the same shape as the pieces in Plate 5. Note that it has the same sturdy, scalloped foot. The pheasant decal suggests this piece might have been part of a game set.

Plate 7: Anchor 104. This creamer in a plain style was found in the East Liverpool area.

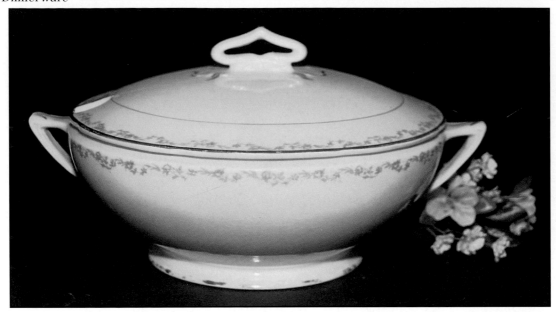

Plate 8: Anchor 105. This tureen has embossing only around the finial. The finial itself consists of a flattened open loop that rises to a well-defined point.

ANCHOR

Baker, 8"	$10.00 – 14.00	Jug, 5 pt.	$40.00 – 50.00
Baker, 9"	$12.00 – 16.00	Nappy, 8"	$12.00 – 16.00
Baker, 10"	$14.00 – 18.00	Nappy, 9"	$14.00 – 18.00
Bone Dish	$5.00 – 7.00	Nappy, 10"	$16.00 – 20.00
Bowl, deep, 1 pt.	$8.00 – 12.00	Oatmeal, 6"	$5.00 – 7.00
Bowl, deep, 1½ pt.	$12.00 – 14.00	Pickle	$12.00 – 16.00
Butter, covered	$40.00 – 50.00	Plate (Coupe Soup), 8"	$7.00 – 8.00
Butter, individual	$3.50 – 5.00	Plate, 6"	$4.50 – 5.50
Casserole, covered,	$30.00 – 45.00	Plate, 7"	$5.50 – 7.00
Coffee Cup	$8.00 – 10.00	Plate, 8"	$6.50 – 8.00
Coffee Saucer	$4.00 – 6.00	Plate, 9"	$8.00 – 9.00
Coffee Saucer, AD	$4.00 – 6.00	Plate, 10"	$9.00 – 10.00
Coffee Cup, AD	$12.00 – 14.00	Plate, deep (Rim Soup), 9"	$8.00 – 9.00
Covered Dish	$30.00 – 40.00	Sauce Boat	$16.00 – 18.00
Creamer	$10.00 – 14.00	Sauce Boat (Fast Stand)	$20.50 – 24.00
Dish (Platter), 11"	$14.00 – 18.00	Sauce Boat Stand	$6.00 – 8.00
Dish (Platter), 13"	$16.00 – 20.00	Sugar, covered	$14.00 – 18.00
Dish (Platter), 15"	$20.00 – 24.00	Teacup (only)	$4.00 – 5.00
Dish (Platter), 17"	$24.00 – 28.00	Teacup Saucer (only)	$2.00 – 3.50
Egg Cup,	$14.50 – 16.00	Teapot	$45.00 – 65.00
Fruit, 5"	$4.00 – 6.00	Tureen	$40.00 – 50.00
Jug, ½ pt.	$14.00 – 18.00	Tureen Ladle	$18.00 – 24.00
Jug, 1 pt.	$18.00 – 24.00	Tureen Stand	$8.50 – 12.00
Jug, 3¼ pt.	$30.00 – 40.00		

The C.C. Thompson Pottery Company was another of the East Liverpool potters, beginning operations in the 1860s in East Liverpool as Thompson and Herbert. The company initially produced Rockingham and yellow ware. In 1870 Josiah Thompson, together with Basil Simms, bought out the intrests of the other owners, and the company became known by the more familiar name of C.C. Thompson and Company.

The firm increased production during the late 1870s and early 1880s, employing 200 workers and operating five kilns. In 1883 or 1884 the firm began making a cream colored ware called "c.c. ware." At that time, the company offered tableware, bedpans, spittoons, and toilet sets.

Josiah Thompson died in 1889, at which time the company was incorporated as the C.C. Thompson Pottery Company. White ironstone toilet wares and dinnerware were added to the company's product line. After World War I the company ceased production of its earlier lines of yellow ware, Rockingham, and c.c. ware in favor of semiporcelain dinnerware. These wares can be seen in advertisements in the Sears catalog of 1938.

Toward the end of 1938 the company fell victim to the wretched business climate and ceased operation forever. For those enthusiasts who are able to make the journey to East Liverpool, the home of Josiah Thompson still stands, where it is being restored by the local historical society.

No figures have become available to reflect the production of the C.C. Thompson pottery during its lifetime. The old pictures of the plant which are seen in its advertisements appear to show around ten kilns. The photograph of the Thompson factory in Plate 9 is prominently dated 1911.

Despite the fact the Thompson house has been turned inside out for catalog information, only one catalog, showing the Eureka shape, has turned up. On the bonus side, they seem to have put the shape name on the back of much of their china, so it is possible to identify many of these shapes even without catalogs. C.C. Thompson wares are encountered in antiques stores often enough to reward the collector willing to take the time to look for them.

Plate 9: The C.C. Thompson & Co. pottery, from an original photograph in the files of the East Liverpool Museum of Ceramics, 1911.

Plate 10: C.C. Thompson 100 (left). Small covered jug with yellow and orange flowers. C.C. Thompson 101 (right). Large covered jug with nasturtiums in orange and yellow. Both these jugs were found in the Ohio area.

C.C. THOMPSON

Covered Jug, large.....$35.00 – 45.00
Covered Jug, small ....$18.00 – 28.00

ALADDIN

Although no catalog pictures are available showing the different pieces making up the Aladdin shape, one can still identify examples that are found in the antiques markets by means of the Aladdin backstamp. (See plate 11.)

Description of points to look for: Aladdin is a simple, business-like shape, with no embossing. The hollow ware emphasizes this theme with a well-defined foot and smooth, outward sloping sides. Handles are utilitarian loops. The flatware pieces come in rounds and ovals with smooth edges unbroken by scallops or indentations.

For suggested values use guide on page 16 and add 10%.

Plate 11: Aladdin backstamp. While this mark is not listed in either Gates and Ormerod or DeBolt, other similar backstamps have been dated from 1905 – 1938.

Plate 12: Aladdin 100. Sauce boat and sauce boat stand with exotic bird decal and orange fluorescent glaze.

Plate 13: Aladdin 101. 7" plate with yellow flowers and black leaves.

FRANCIS

Like most of the American potters of the period, C.C. Thompson produced an imitation of the French Haviland shape called Ranson. C.C. Thompson's answer was the Francis shape, pictured below. Serving pieces are easy to find and a set of plates with colorful fruits decorations was recently purchased from an auction house in Paw Paw, Michigan.

Description of points to look for: See the closeup of the embossing on the Francis shape in Plate 16. The flatware has a scalloped edge.

For suggested values, use guide on page 16.

Plate 14: Francis 100. Nappie with a very attractive decal of a yellow bird sitting on a branch with bright orange flowers. In the Francis shape serving pieces have been the easiest to find. All that I have found are nicely decorated and carry the Francis backstamp.

Plate 15: C.C. Thompson, Francis backstamp dated by Gates and Ormerod[1] as 1916 to 1938.

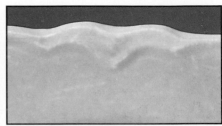

Plate 16: Close-up of the embossing on the Francis shape.

Plate 17: Francis 101. 11" dish (platter) with pastel pink flowers. Francis 102. Salad bowl with large roses.

MADISON

The Madison backstamp is dated from 1916 to 1938 by Gates and Ormerod[1]. Like other C.C. Thompson shapes, many pieces of Madison have the shape name on the back. This is fortunate, since no catalog pages have been found which would show us what Madison looked like. Examples I have found are of good quality with attractive decorations. Aside from a complete set located at the Thompson House in East Liverpool, the Madison shape seems to appear only as individual items: a plate here, a bowl there.

Description of points to look for: Madison is characterized by an octagonal theme which is carried out on all the pieces. Notice that the sugar has a round flat finial. We are probably safe in assuming that the casserole and covered dish also have a like finial. The handles are ear-shaped with a flat top. The most striking feature of this shape is its gadroon edge (see Plate 18 for a good look at this rope-like edge).

For suggested values, use guide on page 16.

Plate 18: Madison 100. 10" plate and deep bowl with a very interesting peacock and flower decal. These pieces were found in the Southern California area.

Plate 20: Madison 101. This set is currently located in the C.C. Thompson House in East Liverpool, Ohio.

EUREKA

Gates and Ormerod[1] date the Eureka backstamp to 1915. The catalog picture below (the only catalog I found for C.C. Thompson) shows a heavily embossed shape with a solid foot and a scalloped edge. Of the two pieces that were found with the Eureka backstamp, one was of poor quality and the embossing was difficult to see. The second was somewhat better and the tiny beaded embossing around the rim was much more in evidence.

For suggested values, use guide on page 16.

Eureka

Plate 21: Eureka backstamp. Note that the Eureka backstamp does not contain the name of the pottery. It would thus be quite easy to overlook pieces of this shape as being made by C.C. Thompson.

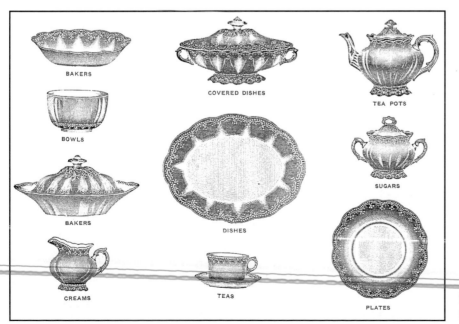

BAKERS

COVERED DISHES

TEA POTS

BOWLS

SUGARS

BAKERS

DISHES

CREAMS

TEAS

PLATES

Plate 22: The Eureka shape, from the files of the East Liverpool Museum of Ceramics.

EUREKA
ALADDIN, FRANCIS, and MADISON

Baker, 5"	$10.00	Dish (Platter), 16"	$22.00
Baker, 6	$12.00	Egg Cup, double	$16.50
Baker, 7"	$14.00	Fruit, 5"	$5.00
Baker, 8"	$16.00	Fruit, 6"	$7.00
Baker, 9"	$18.00	Ice Cream Plate	$18.00
Baker, 10"	$20.00	Jug, 42s (small)	$18.00
Bone Dish	$8.00	Jug, 36s (sm-Med)	$22.00
Bowl, deep, 1 pt.	$12.00	Jug, 24s (medium)	$25.00
Bowl, deep, 1½ pt.	$14.00	Jug, 12s (large)	$40.00
Bowl, oyster, 1 pt.	$10.00	Jug, 6s (ex-large)	$50.00
Bowl, oyster, 1½ pt.	$12.00	Nappy, 8"	$16.00
Butter, covered	$45.00	Nappy, 9"	$18.00
Butter, individual	$5.00	Nappy, 10"	$20.00
Bread Plate	$35.00	Oatmeal, 6"	$6.00
Cake Plate	$20.00	Oatmeal, 6½"	$7.00
Casserole, covered, 8"	$35.00	Pickle	$18.00
Casserole, covered, 9"	$40.00	Plate (Coupe Soup), 7"	$7.00
Casserole, notched lid	$45.00	Plate (Coupe Soup), 8"	$8.00
Coffee Cup	$12.00	Plate (Coupe Soup), 9"	$9.00
Coffee Saucer	$7.00	Plate, 6"	$4.50
Coffee Saucer, AD	$6.00	Plate, 7"	$5.50
Coffee, AD	$14.00	Plate, 8"	$8.50
Covered Dish, 8"	$35.00	Plate, 9"	$9.00
Covered Dish, 9"	$40.00	Plate, 10"	$10.00
Creamer	$12.00	Plate, deep (Rim Soup), 9"	$9.00
Dish (Platter), 6"	$8.00	Salad Bowl (low)	$20.00
Dish (Platter), 7"	$11.00	Salad Bowl (round)	$25.00
Dish (Platter), 8"	$12.00	Sauce Boat	$18.00
Dish (Platter), 9"	$13.00	Sugar	$18.00
Dish (Platter), 10"	$14.00	Teacup (only)	$5.00
Dish (Platter), 11"	$15.00	Teacup Saucer (only)	$3.00
Dish (Platter), 12"	$16.00	Teapot	$65.00
Dish (Platter), 13"	$17.50	Oyster Tureen Stand	$15.00
Dish (Platter), 14"	$19.00	Oyster Tureen, covered	$55.00

East Liverpool Potteries Company

The East Liverpool Potteries Company was a short-lived association of several East Liverpool district potters who banded together to more effectively compete with the larger and more successful firms in the area, such as Homer Laughlin and Knowles, Taylor, Knowles. The East Liverpool Potteries Company was founded in 1901 by combining the following potteries from East Liverpool: Globe; Wallace and Chetwynd; East Liverpool Pottery (note the singular "Pottery"); George C. Murphy; East End Pottery; and The United States Pottery Company (of Wellsville, Ohio).

The East Liverpool Potteries Company appears to have been a rather loose association. Lois Lehner says that the association used a uniform mark, but that the individual companies also continued to produce wares which carried their own marks. Two years after the company was assembled, it began to disintegrate. The East Liverpool Pottery Company left, forming the now-famous Hall China Company. Wallace and Chetwynd never again made china. The East End Pottery Company resumed independent operation until 1909, when they became the Trenle China Company. The George C. Murphy Pottery survived the failure of the association, only to have their plant destroyed by fire a year later, a disaster from which they never recovered.

Globe and United States Pottery continued to operate as East Liverpool Potteries Company until 1907, when Globe left to resume independent operation until 1912. The United States Pottery of Wellsville continued to make wares which carried the East Liverpool Potteries Company mark until it closed its own doors in 1932, undoubtedly a victim of the Great Depression.

During its brief lifetime, the East Liverpool Potteries Company made high quality dinnerware bearing lavish decorations. When one considers the short time that the East Liverpool Potteries Company was in operation, it is a wonder that any pieces at all have survived to the present time. However, pieces bearing the easily recognized shield mark are sometimes found in antiques shops today. After the association broke up, the wares were identified with the much simpler "ELPCO" mark, generally found on pieces which are more ordinary in appearance.

Due both to their quality and their short period of manufacture, pieces bearing the shield mark should be especially treasured. On the following pages can be seen both the catalogs and advertisements that were published when this beautiful china was first sold and photos of pieces that have been located in the antiques markets around the country.

For suggested values, use specialties guide on page 21.

THREE-PIECE SET

FANCY NAPPY

BROTH BOWL

SHELL SALAD

Plates 23, 24, and *25:* Pictures of East Liverpool Potteries specialities from the 1902 *China, Glass and Lamps,* a china trade magazine.

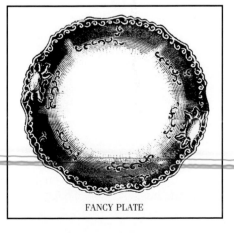

FANCY PLATE

Plate 26: East Liverpool Potteries 100. Fancy bowl with bunches of pink, yellow, and white flowers and gold trimmed embossing.

EAST LIVERPOOL POTTERIES DINNERWARE

Dinnerware produced by East Liverpool Potteries with the old shield mark is today quite rare, not surprising in view of the short life of the company, and the almost 100 years that have elapsed since this china was made. For some unexplainable reason, biscuit jars of all pieces seem to turn up regularly in the antiques markets.

For suggested values, use guide on page 20.

Plate 27: East Liverpool Potteries 105. Biscuit jar with small yellow flowers with a scroll-type embossing. East Liverpool Potteries 106. Cake plate in pink and white. The cake plate is covered with scroll-type embossing very similar to what that seen on the biscuit jar and has a scalloped edge.

Plate 28: East Liverpool Potteries 107. The teapot is a delightful example of the work of this short-lived group of potters. While reflecting the Victorian style and decorating taste, it is not over-done. The otherwise plain sides of the body are broken up with an impressed pattern of vertical folds. The handle and finial are decorated with the usual heavy embossing. Embossing on the lid is outlined in gold, and the entire piece is finished off with tasteful floral decals applied to the side and the lid.

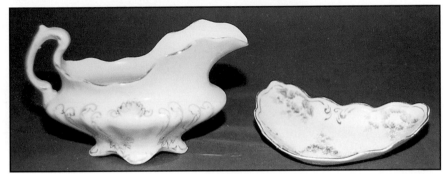

Plate 29: East Liverpool Potteries 108. A sauce boat and bone dish whose shape is similar to the teapot pictured above.

ELPCO

The ELPCO shape was made by the United States Pottery Co., one of the companies which was originally part of the East Liverpool Potteries Co. They continued to use that name after East Liverpool Potteries Co. had closed its doors forever. It has been included in this section since the advertisement shown in Plate 31 still uses the name of the old pottery.

This semivitreous china was a very plain, simple shape with no embossing. The plate and saucer appearing in Plate 33 show a definite rim. The hollow ware has a small foot and a handle-type finial. Handles on the sugar and creamer are a looped circle.

For suggested values, use low side of guide on page 20.

Plate 30: Backstamp found on the ELPCO sugar in Plate 32.

Plate 31: This advertisement for ELPCO was in the files at the East Liverpool Museum. Unfortunately it was just the single page and was not dated.

Plate 32: ELPCO 100. Covered sugar, white with gold trim.

EAST LIVERPOOL POTTERIES

Baker, 8"..................................$14.00 – 18.00	Jug, 3¼ pt.............................$35.00 – 45.00
Baker, 9"..................................$16.00 – 20.00	Jug, 5 pt. ....$40.00 – 55.00
Baker, 10"................................$18.00 – 24.00	Nappy, 8"..............................$14.00 – 18.00
Bone Dish................................$6.00 – 8.00	Nappy, 9" ....$16.00 – 20.00
Bowl, deep, 1 pt.....................$10.00 – 14.00	Nappy, 10" ....$18.00 – 24.00
Bowl, deep, 1½ pt. ....$12.00 – 16.00	Oatmeal.................................$6.00 – 8.00
Butter, covered ....$40.00 – 55.00	Pickle ....$14.00 – 24.00
Butter, individual ....$4.50 – 6.00	Plate (Coupe Soup)...................$7.00 – 9.00
Casserole, covered...............$40.00 – 55.00	Plate, 6"..................................$4.50 – 6.00
Coffee Cup ....$8.00 – 10.00	Plate, 7"..................................$5.50 – 7.00
Coffee Saucer ....$5.00 – 7.00	Plate, 8"..................................$7.00 – 8.50
Coffee Saucer, AD....................$5.00 – 7.00	Plate, 9"..................................$8.00 – 10.00
Coffee Cup, AD ....$13.00 – 16.00	Plate, 10"................................$10.00 – 12.00
Comport ....$55.00 – 75.00	Plate, deep (Rim Soup) ....$8.00 – 10.00
Covered Dish ....$35.00 – 50.00	Sauce Boat ....$18.00 – 22.00
Creamer...................................$12.00 – 14.00	Sauce Boat (Fast Stand) ....$22.50 – 25.00
Dish (Platter), 8" ....$10.00 – 12.00	Sauce Boat Stand ....$8.00 – 10.00
Dish (Platter), 9" ....$12.00 – 14.00	Sauce Tureen ....$35.00 – 40.00
Dish (Platter), 11" ....$14.00 – 16.00	Sauce Tureen, Stand ....$10.00 – 12.00
Dish (Platter), 13" ....$16.00 – 18.00	Sauce Tureen, Ladle ....$22.00 – 24.00
Dish (Platter), 15" ....$20.00 – 24.00	Sugar, covered ....$16.00 – 18.00
Dish (Platter), 17" ....$24.00 – 28.00	Teacup (only) ....$5.00 – 7.00
Dish (Platter), 19" ....$26.00 – 32.00	Teacup Saucer (only) ....$2.50 – 4.00
Egg Cup ....$15.50 – 18.00	Teapot.....................................$55.00 – 75.00
Fruit ....$4.00 – 6.00	Tureen, Soup..........................$55.00 – 80.00
Jug, ½ pt.................................$18.00 – 22.00	Tureen, Soup, Ladle ....$24.00 – 26.00
Jug, 1 pt. ....$22.00 – 25.00	

EAST LIVERPOOL POTTERIES SPECIALTIES

Like other potters from the time, East Liverpool Potteries made specialty items in addition to ordinary dinnerware. The plates shown below are fancy enough to be specialty items. On the other hand, they could also have been part of an elaborate dinner set.

Plate 33: East Liverpool Potteries 101 (Left). Plate with a scalloped edge, a light scroll or vine embossing, and grapes and plums in the center. East Liverpool Potteries 102 (Right). Plate with a scalloped edge, indentation that runs around the rim, and a pair of colorful birds.

Plate 34: East Liverpool Potteries 103. Plaque with heavy embossing and large yellow roses and violets in the center.

Plate 35: East Liverpool Potteries 104. Plaque titled Pope Leo.

EAST LIVERPOOL POTTERIES SPECIALTIES

Fancy or advertising plate .....$20.00 – 30.00	Fancy Nappy.........................$18.00 – 28.00
Plaques...............................$25.00 – 35.00	Broth Bowl...........................$12.00 – 14.00
Three-piece Tea Set ....$75.00 – 85.00	Shell Salad...........................$30.00 – 40.00

East Liverpool Pottery Company

The East Liverpool Pottery Company was founded in East Liverpool, Ohio, in 1894 by John W. Hall, Robert Hall, and Monroe Patterson. For two years the company produced plain and decorated ironstone china, but in 1896 they switched to the manufacture of semivitreous china. Five years later the company joined with five other potteries to form the East Liverpool Potteries Company, which has its own section in this book.

Pieces made by the East Liverpool Pottery Company are quite rare today. I have found only four pieces myself, all of them later semivitreous wares. Two of these carry the shield mark, and to me feel much more massive than the other two, which carry the "WACO" mark. Whether this implies the general use of the "WACO" mark on more elegant pieces or not, I cannot determine. However, this is a mystery that certainly lends itself to solution by you, the individual collectors and dealers, which is part of the fun of collecting these old dishes.

It is important to not confuse this pottery with the East Liverpool Potteries Company, which used different marks.

Plate 36: East Liverpool Pottery 100. Sauce boat of an unidentified shape with the shield backstamp similar to the one seen below, but without the word: "Narcissus." Note that this shape has smooth edges and no embossing.

NARCISSUS

The Narcissus shape is dated by Gates and Ormerod[1] as 1896 to 1901. For suggested values, use guide on page 24.

Plate 37: Narcissus 100. This relish is the only example I have of the Narcissus shape. Look for the Narcissus mark on the back, rather than trying to identify other examples of Narcisson by comparison to this piece. The relish dish was usually quite different from the other pieces.

Plate 38: East Liverpool Pottery Co., Narcissus shape, backstamp.

WACO

Waco was not really a shape name, but the trade name for a type of china manufactured by the East Liverpool Pottery Company. Both of the pieces shown below look like they may be the same shape. Both have deep line embossing, scallops on the edges, and handles that are ear-shaped with nubs on the bottom (where the earring would go) and a nub on the top. Waco was made briefly, from 1896 to 1901. Both its short production run and its antiquity have made Waco a seldom-seen mark today.

For suggested values, use guide on page 24.

Plate 39: East Liverpool Pottery Co., WACO, backstamp.

Plate 40: WACO 100. Sauce boat, white with blue flowers and WACO backstamp.

Plate 41: WACO 101. Covered dish with very attractive purple color and WACO backstamp.

EAST LIVERPOOL POTTERY COMPANY
NARCISSUS and WACO

Baker, 8"	$10.00 – 14.00	Jug, 5 pt.	$40.00 – 50.00
Baker, 9"	$12.00 – 16.00	Nappy, 8"	$12.00 – 16.00
Baker, 10"	$14.00 – 18.00	Nappy, 9"	$14.00 – 18.00
Bone Dish	$5.00 – 7.00	Nappy, 10"	$16.00 – 20.00
Bowl, deep, 1 pt.	$8.00 – 12.00	Oatmeal, 6"	$5.00 – 7.00
Bowl, deep, 1 pt.	$12.00 – 14.00	Pickle	$12.00 – 16.00
Butter, covered	$40.00 – 50.00	Plate (Coupe Soup), 8"	$7.00 – 8.00
Butter, individual	$3.50 – 5.00	Plate, 6"	$4.50 – 5.50
Casserole, covered	$30.00 – 45.00	Plate, 7"	$5.50 – 7.00
Coffee Cup	$8.00 – 10.00	Plate, 8"	$6.50 – 8.00
Coffee Saucer	$4.00 – 6.00	Plate, 9"	$8.00 – 9.00
Coffee Saucer, AD	$4.00 – 6.00	Plate, 10"	$9.00 – 10.00
Coffee Cup, AD	$12.00 – 14.00	Plate, deep (Rim Soup), 9"	$8.00 – 9.00
Covered Dish	$30.00 – 40.00	Sauce Boat	$16.00 – 18.00
Creamer	$10.00 – 14.00	Sauce Boat (Fast Stand)	$20.50 – 24.00
Dish (Platter), 11"	$14.00 – 18.00	Sauce Boat Stand	$6.00 – 8.00
Dish (Platter), 13"	$16.00 – 20.00	Sugar, covered	$14.00 – 18.00
Dish (Platter), 15"	$20.00 – 24.00	Teacup (only)	$4.00 – 5.00
Dish (Platter), 17"	$24.00 – 28.00	Teacup Saucer (only)	$2.00 – 3.50
Egg Cup	$14.50 – 16.00	Teapot	$45.00 – 65.00
Fruit, 5"	$4.00 – 6.00	Tureen	$40.00 – 50.00
Jug, pt.	$14.00 – 18.00	Tureen Ladle	$18.00 – 24.00
Jug, 1 pt.	$18.00 – 24.00	Tureen Stand	$8.50 – 12.00
Jug, 3 pt.	$30.00 – 40.00		

East Palestine Pottery Co. & W.S. George Pottery Co.

The East Palestine Pottery Company could well be the recipient of the title: "Most Named China Company." The company was founded in East Palestine, Ohio, in 1880, to make yellow ware and Rockingham. In 1881, the company was known as the Feustal and Knowling Pottery Company. However, three years later, the name was changed to the more familiar East Palestine Pottery Company when it was sold to a group of potters from nearby East Liverpool, Ohio. In 1889 the company was incorporated, the plant was enlarged, and production of white and decorated wares commenced. Four years later, in 1893, the company found itself again on the brink of financial ruin.

George Sebring was hired as manager. Sebring put the company on a paying basis, and in 1896 he left to found the Ohio China Company.

The company continued to enjoy the name East Palestine Pottery Company until 1904, when a controlling interest in the plant was purchased by W.S. George. George built a new plant adjacent to the existing East Palestine Pottery works. The new plant was called the Continental China Company. Five years later the two plants were merged under the well-known name of W. S. George. At about that same time another W.S. George Pottery was started in Canonsburg, Pennsylvania. On top of all of this, in 1913 W.S. George took over the Pennsylvania China Co., of Kittanning, Pennsylvania, so that he now owned four potteries, two in East Palestine, one in Canonsburg, and the last in Kittanning.

Today, wares bearing marks of both EPPCO and W.S. George are found, although many more of the latter than the former.

For suggested values, use guide on page 28.

Plate 42: One of the East Palestine backstamps: dated ca. 1895 to ca. 1905 by Gerald DeBolt.[2]

Plate 43: An advertisement in the March 8, 1928, issue of *The Pottery, Glass & Brass Salesman* shows the four W.S. George potteries: Plants 1 and 4 in East Liverpool, Ohio; Plant 2 at Canonsburg, Pennsylvania; and Plant 3 in Kittanning, Pennsylvania.

IRIS

The Iris shape, made first by the East Palestine Company in 1905, was continued until 1920 after the name of the pottery was changed to W. S. George. Today, pieces of Iris are moderately easy to find in the antique market, probably due to the long production life of this shape.

Description of points to look for: The Iris flatware has a scalloped edge and both hollow ware and flatware have a bead embossing around the rim. The catalog pictures show a leaf-like embossing around the rim under the lines of beads; however, on the platter I found the embossing to be very faint and difficult to see. Finials on the hollow ware have a flattened oval look; the handles are slightly embossed.

Value guide on page 28.

Plate 44: Picture of the Iris backstamp used by the East Palestine Pottery Company. Gerald DeBolt[2] dates this as 1905 to 1909. Note that Iris with the W.S. George name and logo was continued after the name change around 1910.

Plate 45: Iris 100. Dish (platter), 17½". This platter carried the older East Palestine Iris backstamp.

Plate 46: Iris 101. Casserole from the collection of Frederick Morth.

Plates 47 and 48: Some items made in the Iris shape pictured in a catalog at the East Liverpool Museum of Ceramics.

IRIS

EAST PALESTINE POTTERY CO., W.S. GEORGE POTTERY CO., and DESOTO.

Baker, 6	$12.00	Fruit, 5"	$5.00
Baker, 7"	$14.00	Fruit, 5½"	$6.00
Baker, 8"	$16.00	Fruit, 6"	$7.00
Baker, 9"	$18.00	Jug, ½ pt.	$16.00
Baker, 10"	$22.00	Jug, ¾ pt.	$20.00
Baker, 11"	$24.00	Jug, 1½ pt.	$30.00
Bone Dish	$6.00	Jug, 2½ pt.	$35.00
Bouillon Cup	$12.00	Jug, 4 pt.	$40.00
Bouillon Saucer	$4.00	Jug, 5 pt.	$45.00
Bowl, deep, 1 pt.	$11.00	Jug, 6 pt.	$50.00
Bowl, deep, 2 pt.	$13.00	Nappy, 6½"	$12.00
Bowl, deep, 3 pt.	$15.00	Nappy, 7½"	$14.00
Butter, covered	$50.00	Nappy, 8½"	$16.00
Butter, individual	$5.50	Nappy, 9½"	$18.00
Cake Plate	$25.00	Nappy, 10½"	$20.00
Casserole, covered	$40.00	Nappy, 11½"	$24.00
Casserole, notched lid	$45.00	Oatmeal, 6"	$7.00
Celery Tray	$25.00	Pickle	$18.00
Coffee Cup	$12.00	Plate (Coupe Soup), 7½"	$7.00
Coffee Saucer	$6.00	Plate (Coupe Soup), 8"	$8.00
Coffee Saucer, AD	$6.00	Plate (Coupe Soup), 9½"	$9.00
Coffee, AD	$14.00	Plate, 6"	$4.50
Covered Dish	$35.00	Plate, 7"	$5.50
Creamer	$12.00	Plate, 8"	$8.50
Custard, handled	$18.00	Plate, 9"	$9.00
Custard, unhandled	$15.00	Plate, 10"	$10.00
Dish (Platter), 7"	$11.00	Plate, deep (Rim Soup), 8"	$8.00
Dish (Platter), 8"	$12.00	Plate, deep (Rim Soup), 9"	$9.00
Dish (Platter), 9"	$13.00	Sauce Boat	$18.00
Dish (Platter), 10"	$14.00	Sauce Boat Stand	$9.00
Dish (Platter), 11"	$16.00	Sherbet	$22.00
Dish (Platter), 12"	$18.00	Spoon Holder	$45.00
Dish (Platter), 13"	$20.50	Sugar	$18.00
Dish (Platter), 14"	$24.00	Sugar, individual	$14.00
Dish (Platter), 16"	$28.00	Teacup (only)	$5.00
Dish (Platter), 17½"	$30.00	Teacup Saucer (only)	$3.00
Egg Cup, double	$16.50	Teapot	$70.00

DESOTO

A 1904 issue of *China, Glass and Lamps* talks about East Palestine's new "Desoto" shape. Since catalog pictures could not be found for this shape, it is fortunate that most of the pieces have "Desoto" in the backstamp. DeSoto is not as plentiful as Iris.

From the dinnerware pieces found, here are some of the most distinctive features: The flatware has a scalloped edge and light embossing. The ends of the platters almost come to a point and the hollow ware pieces are rounded in an almost pumpkin-like shape. The handle that we can see on the jug in Plate 52 is slightly embossed and seems to lie on the surface of the jug where it connects at the bottom, somewhat like it was glued on.

For suggested values, use the Iris shape on page 28.

Plate 49: Desoto 100. This looks like a relish dish. It hardly seems to go with the rest of the Desoto shape pieces, but many old style sets had relish or pickle dishes that were very different from the rest of the set.

Plate 51: The EPPCO Desoto backstamp found on all the pieces pictured here. It is not known if Desoto was continued after the W.S. George backstamp came into use.

Plate 50: Desoto 101. Fruit bowl with violet decal.

Plate 52: Desoto 102. 14" dish (platter). Desoto 103. Jug with rose decal.

ARGOSY

Dated from the late 1920s, this shape with its unusual handles is easy to identify. For values use Radisson guide on page 32.

Plate 53: One of the Argosy backstamps.

Plate 54: Argosy 100. Sugar. Argosy 101. Two pint jug.

RADISSON

A quote from the April 1942 *China and Glass* magazine, in an article titled "Anne Visits the W.S. George Showrooms," says: "at least two of the early George designs have gone on steadily selling for no less a time than 35 years. One is a scalloped, slightly embossed shape called Radisson." This would place the start of Radisson production at least back to 1907. However, DeBolt[2] places the Radisson mark back only to 1910, after the name of the pottery changed to W.S. George. In any event, both sources place the start of production in the first decade of this century. Not surprisingly, Radisson is quite easy to find today.

Description of points to look for: The Radisson is W.S. George's take-off on the familiar Haviland shape. The finials and handles have a crinkled appearance. The handle of the cup is smooth, which may make it easy to hold, but it seems a bit out of place in this set with otherwise very fancy handles. The flatware has scalloped edges.

For suggested values, use guide on page 32.

Plate 55: Radisson backstamp.

Plate 56: Radisson 100, 14" dish (platter), casserole, cups and saucer, creamer, sauce boat, and relish or sauce boat stand. This set, except for the creamer, was sent to me from Michigan. The creamer came from Florida. I have also seen a large set in the same pattern in my Southern California area. It seems that the Radisson shape may be found in many different places in the United States.

RADISSON

Baker, 6"	$8.00	Fruit, 5½"	$5.00
Baker, 6½"	$10.00	Fruit, 6"	$7.00
Baker, 7½"	$12.00	Jug, ½ pt.	$16.00
Baker, 8½"	$14.00	Jug, ¾ pt.	$20.00
Baker, 9½"	$16.00	Jug, 1 pt.	$25.00
Baker, 10"	$18.00	Jug, 2 pt.	$30.00
Baker, 11"	$20.00	Jug, 3 pt.	$35.00
Bone Dish	$6.00	Jug, 4 pt.	$45.00
Bouillon Cup	$12.00	Jug, 5 pt.	$50.00
Bouillon Saucer	$4.00	Nappy, 6"	$12.00
Bowl, deep, 1 pt.	$12.00	Nappy, 7"	$14.00
Bowl, deep, 1½ pt.	$15.00	Nappy, 8"	$16.00
Bowl, deep, 2 pt.	$18.00	Nappy, 9"	$18.00
Bowl, oyster, 1½ pt.	$14.00	Nappy, 10"	$20.00
Butter, covered	$50.00	Nappy, 11"	$24.00
Butter, individual	$5.50	Oatmeal, 6"	$7.00
Cake Plate	$25.00	Pickle	$16.00
Casserole, covered	$40.00	Plate (Coupe Soup), 7½"	$7.00
Casserole, notched lid	$45.00	Plate (Coupe Soup), 8"	$8.00
Coffee Cup	$12.00	Plate (Coupe Soup), 9½"	$9.00
Coffee Saucer	$6.00	Plate, 6"	$4.50
Coffee Saucer, AD	$6.00	Plate, 7"	$5.50
Coffee, AD	$14.00	Plate, 8"	$8.50
Covered Dish	$35.00	Plate, 9"	$9.00
Creamer	$12.00	Plate, 10"	$10.00
Custard, handled	$18.00	Plate, deep (Rim Soup), 8"	$8.00
Custard, unhandled	$15.00	Plate, deep (Rim Soup), 9"	$9.00
Dish (Platter), 7"	$11.00	Sauce Boat	$18.00
Dish (Platter), 8"	$12.00	Sauce Boat (Fast Stand)	$24.00
Dish (Platter), 9"	$13.00	Sauce Ladle	$22.00
Dish (Platter), 10"	$14.00	Sauce Tureen Stand	$10.50
Dish (Platter), 11"	$15.00	Sauce Tureen	$35.00
Dish (Platter), 12	$16.00	Sugar	$18.00
Dish (Platter), 13"	$17.50	Sugar, individual	$14.00
Dish (Platter), 14½"	$20.00	Teacup (only)	$5.00
Dish (Platter), 16"	$24.00	Teacup Saucer (only)	$3.00
Dish (Platter), 17½"	$28.00	Teapot	$70.00
Egg Cup, double	$16.50		

Plates 57 and 58: Catalog pictures of Radisson.

DERWOOD

In 1942, *China and Glass* magazine said: "Another shape made and sold for 35 years was Derwood, a plain dinnerware shape." Like the Radisson shape, this would suggest that Derwood was first made right after W.S. George purchased the East Palestine Pottery. The article further talks about patterns seen on Derwood: "Springtime: a delicate little shoulder wreath, Blue Dawn: a laurel pattern in blue, and Rhapsody which is a pink floral border." Today's antique collector will find Derwood to be reasonably plentiful.

When I purchased my first Derwood casserole I thought there might be a mistake. The backstamp said Derwood but the shape of my casserole did not match the casserole in the catalog picture I had copied at the East Liverpool Museum of Ceramics. It took another trip to East Liverpool, some more digging, and another Derwood catalog to come up with the answer. Derwood has not one, not two, but four different styles of hollow ware!

Description of points to look for: Derwood has no embossing. Flatware is round or oval with smooth edges. The different styles of finials and handles are best seen in Plates 63 and 64, which show the different variants of the Derwood hollow ware. It should be noted that while the cup in the catalog pictures shown on page 37 has little or no foot, a later change was made to a footed cup.

For suggested values, use guide on page 36.

Plate 59: Derwood backstamp.

Plate 60: Derwood 100. 7" plate with pink roses on a black background, inset into a blue band. Derwood 101. A covered dish decorated with a garland of pink and blue flowers.

Plate 61: Derwood 102. 9" plate and 5 pint water pitcher decorated with a narrow band in black with pink flowers. [From the collection of Susan Cenfetelle.]

Plate 62: This Derwood covered jug strongly resembles the Ohio jugs made by Edwin Knowles.

Plates 63 and 64: Examples of different styles of Derwood hollow ware.

Derwood

Baker, 5½"..$8.00	Jug, ¾ pt. $16.00
Baker, 6" $10.00	Jug, 1 pt. $20.00
Baker, 7" $12.00	Jug, 1½ pt. $24.00
Baker, 8" $14.00	Jug, 2½ pt. $30.00
Baker, 9" $16.00	Jug, 3½ pt. $35.00
Baker, 10" $18.00	Jug, 5 pt. $40.00
Baker, 11" $20.00	Jug, 6½ pt. $45.00
Bone Dish...$6.00	Jug, covered, ¾ pt. $24.00
Bouillon Cup..$12.00	Jug, covered, 1 pt. $28.00
Bouillon Saucer $4.00	Jug, covered, 1½ pt. $34.00
Bowl, deep, 1 pt. $11.00	Jug, covered, 2½ pt. $40.00
Bowl, deep, 1½ pt. $12.00	Jug, covered, 3½ pt. $45.00
Bowl, deep, 2 pt. $14.00	Jug, covered, 5 pt. $55.00
Bowl, oyster, 1½ pt..................................$10.00	Muffin Dish..$45.00
Butter, covered $45.00	Nappy, 6" $12.00
Butter, individual $5.50	Nappy, 7" $14.00
Cake Plate...$20.00	Nappy, 8" $16.00
Casserole, covered $40.00	Nappy, 9" $18.00
Casserole, notched lid $45.00	Nappy, 10" $20.00
Chop Dish..$20.00	Nappy, 11" $24.00
Coffee Cup...$10.00	Oatmeal, 6½"...$7.00
Coffee Saucer $6.00	Pickle..$16.00
Coffee Saucer, AD....................................$6.00	Plate (Coupe Soup), 7½"..........................$7.00
Coffee, AD $13.00	Plate (Coupe Soup), 8" $8.00
Covered Dish $35.00	Plate (Coupe Soup), 9½"..........................$9.00
Creamer $12.00	Plate, 6" $4.50
Cream, individual....................................$10.00	Plate, 7" $5.50
Cream Soup..$16.00	Plate, 8" $8.50
Cream Soup Stand $7.00	Plate, 9" $9.00
Custard, handled $18.00	Plate, 10" $10.00
Custard, unhandled $15.00	Plate, deep (Rim Soup), 8½"..................$8.00
Dish (Platter), 6½" $8.00	Plate, deep (Rim Soup), 9½"..................$9.00
Dish (Platter), 7½" $11.00	Ramekin..$12.00
Dish (Platter), 8½" $12.00	Ramekin Stand $5.00
Dish (Platter), 9½" $13.00	Sauce Boat..$16.50
Dish (Platter), 10½" $14.00	Sauce Boat Stand $9.00
Dish (Platter), 11½" $15.00	Sauce Boat (Fast Stand) $24.00
Dish (Platter), 12½...................................$16.00	Sauce Ladle..$20.00
Dish (Platter), 13½" $17.50	Sauce Tureen Stand $10.00
Dish (Platter), 14½" $20.00	Sauce Tureen...$30.00
Dish (Platter), 16" $24.00	Sugar..$16.50
Dish (Platter), 17½" $28.00	Sugar, individual.....................................$14.00
Egg Cup, double $15.50	Teacup (only)..$5.00
Egg Cup, Boston $22.00	Teacup Saucer (only) $3.00
Fruit, 5"..$5.00	Teapot $55.00
Fruit, 6"..$7.00	

Plates 65 and 66: Catalog pictures of Derwood.

French China Company

The French China Company was organized by the Sebring brothers in East Liverpool, Ohio, in 1898. In East Liverpool, the company made semiporcelain dinner, tea, and toilet wares, as well as "Special Novelties" (Gates). In 1901 the operation was moved to Sebring, Ohio. There they continued to make quality semiporcelain wares. In 1916 O.H. Sebring created the Sebring Manufacturing Company, which acted as a holding company for the French China Company, as well as the Strong Manufacturing Company and the Saxon China Company. However, the French China Company still continued to operate independently. In 1929 the holding company joined the ill-fated American Chinaware Corporation, which failed two years after, terminating the French China Company as well.

During the time it operated, French produced some very elegant pieces, samples of which are frequently found on the antique china market. The wares that are found consist of both dinner-ware items and specialty plates. While the later dinnerware shapes appear to be rather ordinary in appearance, the same cannot be said for the earlier pieces, which are tastefully and lavishly decorated. For several months I admired some small plates which were probably part of a fish set that were for sale in a local antiques mall. They were decorated with finely detailed and life-like decals of fish in the center, while the rims were decorated with a deep blue glaze. However, the seller wanted an outrageous price and refused to negotiate. All thoughts of acquiring (or even photographing) these plates were abruptly terminated on January 17, 1994, when the Northridge earthquake utterly destroyed them. In spite of this loss, the colored plates on the following pages will give the prospective collector of French China wares an example of the delights that will be their reward.

Plate 67: Early French China Company backstamp.

Plate 68: This copy of a picture of the French China Company was taken from letter-head found at the East Liverpool Museum of Ceramics.

Plate 69: French 100. This advertising plate, made for "Berlin Bros." has a decal that is an exceptionally nice example of the "Dutch scene" decals favored at this time. For values of advertising plates see page 46.

LORNA DOONE

Gates and Ormerod date the backstamp that appears on the back of this shape (see Plate 67 on page 38 for a picture of this backstamp) from 1916 to 1920. Gerald DeBolt dates it 1905 to 1915. Since the French China Company neglected to use backstamps which contained dates by which enthusiasts resolve this disagreement. Regardless of the specific dates, Lorna Doone was probably not produced for a very long time, since it has proven to be rather hard to find today.

Description of points to look for: The Lorna Doone shape has flatware with just a hint of a scalloped edge and embossing around the rim that has a fan-like appearance. The coupe soup bowl in Plate 72 provides a detailed view of the Lorna Doone embossing. The hollow ware has just a hint of a foot from which the body flairs out and curves inward to the top. The finials resemble a small open crown and the handles have an almost faceted appearance, both providing a good means of positive identification.

Value guide page 49.

Plate 70: Lorna 100. Creamer and sugar with flow blue decoration on rim and handles. [From the collection of Donna and Bill Gray, Columbia, Maryland.]

Flow blue decoration is highly prized by collectors today, often without regard for the pottery or the underlying shape. Pieces with flow blue decoration should be valued 50% above pieces with normal decorations which are the basis of the value guide.

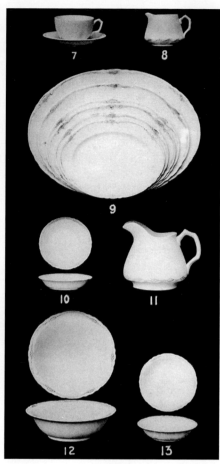

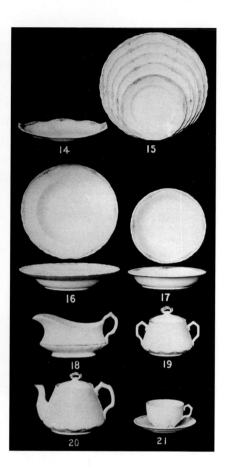

Plate 71: Catalog pictures of Lorna Doone.

1	Baker	7	Coffee & Saucer	12	Nappy	17	Coupe Soup
2	Butter, covered	8	Creamer	13	Oatmeal	18	Sauce Boat
3	Butter, individual	9	Dishes (Platters)	14	Pickle	19	Sugar
4	Casserole	10	Fruit	15	Plates	20	Teapot
5	Bowl, deep	11	Jug	16	Deep Plate (Rim Soup)	21	Teacup & Saucer
6	Covered Dish						

Plate 72: Lorna 101. Coupe soup with decal that resembles a European-style country home in its center.

PRISCILLA

The Priscilla shape appears in the same catalog that describes Lorna Doone. Since both Priscilla and Lorna Doone have been found (in the limited samples seen so far) to use the same backstamp, we are probably safe in assuming they were produced at about the same time.

Description of points to look for: The Priscilla flatware consists of simple rounds and ovals with no embossing. The hollow ware has simple handle-like finials and handles that are similar to a curved triangle. While I have only one piece in my collection so far, it is quite possible that new collectors armed with descriptions of Priscilla will succeed in tracking down other examples of this rare and attractive shape. Below is the one piece that was turned up for me by a friend in West Virginia.

Value guide page 49.

Plate 73: Priscilla 100. Coupe soup bowl ringed with yellow and green flowers.

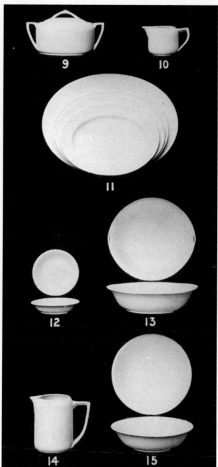
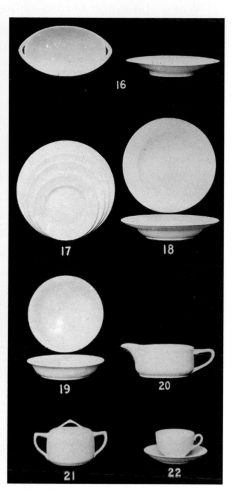

Plate 74: Catalog pictures of Priscilla.

1 Baker	7 Chop Plate	13 Fruit Bowl	19 Coupe Soup
2 Bon Bon	8 Covered Dish	14 Jug	20 Sauce Boat
3 Butter, covered	9 Cracker Jar	15 Nappy	21 Sugar
4 Butter, individual	10 Creamer	16 Pickle	22 Teacup & Saucer
5 Cake Plate	11 Dishes (Platters)	17 Plates	
6 Casserole	12 Fruit	18 Plate, deep (Rim Soup)	

ON EVERY PIECE

LA FRANCAISE

SEMI-PORCELAIN

THE MARK OF QUALITY

Plate 75: Backstamp from Priscilla bowl shown in Plate 72.

MARTHA WASHINGTON

When you come across china from the French China Company, it is most likely to be Martha Washington. The Martha Washington shape must have been very popular due to the many pieces that have been found all over the country.

Description of points to look for: The most striking thing about this shape is its faceted appearance. The rims of the flatware pieces clearly show this effect. The same angular theme is continued in the serving pieces, as can be seen in the casserole in Plate 79. The pieces have a light feel to them and show a good quality of workmanship. However, the gold used to decorate many of the pieces has not stood the test of time and is often severely worn. The glaze used on this shape appears to resist grease poorly, since I have found that sauce boats and casseroles are often severely stained. Fortunately, these stains readily submit to soaking in agents such as strong peroxide, thus surprising the discouraged collector with a piece of china that looks almost new rather than ready for the trash can.

Bill Gates and Dana Ormerod date this shape from 1916 to 1929 which falls in line with an advertisement from the *China, Glass, and Lamps* magazine dated January 1, 1917, announcing: "Martha Washington dinnerware, the new shape put on the market by the French China Company."

Several pieces of Martha Washington have the Sebring Pottery backstamp on them as shown in Plate 77. This is not too surprising since French China was owned by the Sebring Pottery Company.

Value guide page 49.

Plate 76: French China Company, Martha Washington backstamp.

Plate 77: Sebring Pottery Co. Martha Washington backstamp.

Plate 78: Martha 100. Covered dish with doves on a blue background. Martha 102. 7" plate with a parrot on a swing and flowers.

Plate 79: Martha 101. 15" dish (platter) with pink flowers and yellow and black designs. Martha Washington pattern #336. Cup, saucer, and sauce boat with wreaths and garlands of flowers.

SPECIALTY ITEMS

The amount of specialty items made by the French China Company which are found in the antiques markets of today is surprisingly large. Whether this is due to a high rate of manufacture or to a low mortality rate cannot be said. Many of the pieces seen were certainly not for everyday use, so it is possible that they were put up in a cupboard and used only for special occasions, thus allowing them to escape the fate of so much of the old china.

Plate 80: French 100. Two bowls which may have been part of a game set.

SPECIALTY VALUE GUIDE

Salad or Specialty Bowl, 9"...$20.00 – 30.00
Salad or Specialty Bowl, 10"...$25.00 – 35.00
Specialty or Advertising Plate ....$20.00 – 35.00
Fancy Fruit or Ice Cream Tray..$35.00 – 45.00

FISH OR GAME SETS

Dish (Platter) ....$45.00 – 65.00
Plate ....$20.00 – 30.00
Bowl..$25.00 – 35.00

Pieces with flow blue decoration should be valued 50% above pieces with normal decorations which are the basis of the value guide.

Plate 81: French 101. A salad or specialty bowl with lovely luster glaze and large roses.

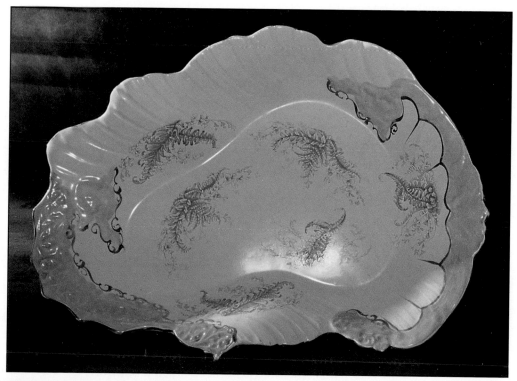

Plate 82: French 102. I think this unusual bowl may be either a fancy fruit bowl or ice cream tray. It seems similar to the one pictured on page 209 from Sebring Pottery, which is the parent company of French China Company.

Plate 83: French 100. This plate with the snowy field and a lurking fox has an attractive flow blue border. For pricing use the specialty price guide on page 46.

Plate 84: French 101. A bowl with a decal of roses and cobalt blue border that may have been a salad bowl or one of the other many specialty bowls made by French China Company. For pricing use the speciality price guide on page 46.

Martha Washington, Priscilla, & Lorna Doone

L – Lorna, P – Priscilla

L Baker, 5½"	$10.00	P Fruit Bowl, 10½" $30.00
Baker, 8"	$14.00	L Jug, 1½ pt. $22.00
Baker, 9"	$16.00	L Jug, 2 pt. $25.00
Baker, 10"	$18.00	Jug, 3¼ pt. $30.00
P Bon Bon, 9½"	$20.00	L Jug, 4 pt. $35.00
P Bon Bon, 10"	$24.00	Jug, 6 pt. $42.00
L Bowl, deep, 1 pt.	$11.00	Nappy, 7" $14.00
L Bowl, deep, 1½ pt.	$13.00	Nappy, 8" $16.00
Butter, covered	$50.00	Nappy, 9" $18.00
Butter, individual	$5.50	L Nappy, 10" $20.00
Cake Plate	$22.00	L Nappy, 11" $24.00
Casserole, covered	$35.00	Oatmeal, 6" $7.00
Chop Plate	$22.00	Pickle $14.00
Coffee Cup	$9.00	Plate (Coupe Soup), 8" $8.00
Coffee Saucer	$6.00	Plate (Coupe Soup), 9" $9.00
Coffee Saucer, AD	$16.00	Plate (Coupe Soup), 9½"...........$10.00
Coffee, AD	$12.00	Plate, 6" $4.50
Covered Dish, 8½"	$35.00	Plate, 7" $5.50
Covered Dish, 9½"	$40.00	Plate, 8" $7.00
Cracker Jar	$55.00	Plate, 9" $8.00
Creamer	$12.00	Plate, 10" $9.00
L Dish (Platter), 9½"	$18.00	Plate, deep (Rim Soup), 9"..........$9.00
Dish (Platter), 10½"	$14.00	Sauce Boat $18.00
Dish (Platter), 11½"	$16.00	Sugar, covered $16.00
Dish (Platter), 12½"	$18.00	Teacup (only) $5.00
Dish (Platter), 13½"	$22.00	Teacup Saucer (only) $3.00
Dish (Platter), 15½"	$25.00	Teapot $65.00
L Dish (Platter), 17½"	$28.00	Tureen $50.00
Fruit, 5"	$5.00	Tureen Ladle...............................$25.00
P Fruit Bowl, 8½"	$25.00	Tureen Stand $12.00

Globe Pottery Company

For the history of the Globe Pottery Company we again turn to Gates and Omerod[1]. Several partners founded the Frederick, Shenkle, Allen and Company in 1881, in East Liverpool. In early 1882 the company began making Rockingham and yellow ware. In 1888 the company was reorganized as the Globe Pottery Company, at which time they added semiporcelain to their product line. By the mid 1890s the company was producing Rockingham, cream colored ware, decorated jet ware and teapots, and specialty items.

In 1901 Globe joined the East Liverpool Potteries Company, but this company ceased operation almost as soon as it was founded. Upon the demise of the East Liverpool Potteries Company, Globe resumed independent operation in 1907 under new management. At this time they produced semiporcelain dinnerware as well as specialty items. The company gradually declined, and finally received a death blow from a flood in 1912.

In spite of its brief lifetime, Globe has provided us with very fine and collectable pieces, some of which can be seen on the pages which follow. Unfortunately a lack of catalog materials or advertisements for Globe products keeps us in the dark as far as the names of the different shapes they produced. In the absence of historical data, we can only assume that they produced a variety of wares which were similar in extent to those of other small potteries of the time.

GLOBE POTTERY CO.
Specialty Plates:.......$15.00 – 25.00.

Plate 85: Globe 100. Specialty plate or plaque with large purple plums and olive green leaves.

Look These Assortments Over

This "Big Noise" assortment contains twenty-five different 10c items, twenty of each. The only 10c assortment with equal quantities of each piece. Decorated in a thin spray decal, with gold stamps between. We will gladly furnish you with a sample and the composition.

This "Nevada Assortment" is just a little bit the best small 10c assortment on the market, containing twenty-two dozen pieces, of which

Six Dozen are 25c Sellers

Our price on this assortment is less than that asked for ordinary 10c assortments. We have samples ready for you. Get our compositions on this winner.

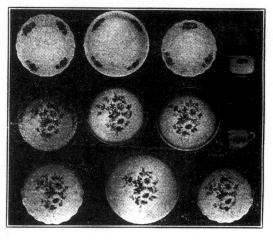

The Globe 25c Assortment is made up in 6 doz and 12 doz packages. This assortment is really a 50c retailer and is sure to strike your fancy. Every item large and well decorated. Try a sample package. We will be pleased to send you the composition.

The Globe Pottery Co. EAST LIVERPOOL. OHIO

Plate 86: Advertisement from the August 14, 1911, *China, Glass, and Lamps* magazine.

ST. REGIS

Like most Globe dinnerware, the St. Regis shape has proven difficult to locate. If it dates from Globe's earlier period (1888 – 1901), age would explain why it is so rare. St. Regis flatware consists of simple rounds and ovals with no embossing. The hollow ware has a very sturdy solid look. Its most outstanding feature is its oblong finial which has a large pointy nub stuck in its center. (See Plate 88.) Value guide on page 53.

Plate 87: Globe backstamp found on the back of the plate shown below. The mark was used both before (1888 – 1901) and after (1907 – 1912) the involvement with East Liverpool Potteries.

Plate 88: St. Regis dinnerware advertisement, from a contemporary trade magazine. [From the East Liverpool Museum of Ceramics.]

Plate 89: St. Regis 100. 7" plate with cherries.

GLOBE

Baker, 8"	$14.00	Jug, 5 pt.	$40.00
Baker, 9"	$18.00	Nappy, 8"	$16.00
Baker, 10"	$22.00	Nappy, 9"	$20.00
Bone Dish	$8.00	Nappy, 10"	$24.00
Bowl, deep, 1 pt.	$13.00	Oatmeal, 6"	$7.00
Bowl, deep, 1½ pt.	$15.00	Pickle	$20.00
Butter, covered	$55.00	Plate (Coupe Soup), 8"	$8.00
Butter, individual	$4.50	Plate, 6"	$5.50
Casserole, covered	$45.00	Plate, 7"	$7.00
Coffee Cup	$10.00	Plate, 8"	$8.00
Coffee Saucer	$6.00	Plate, 9"	$9.00
Coffee Saucer, AD	$6.00	Plate, 10"	$10.00
Coffee Cup, AD	$14.00	Plate, deep (Rim Soup), 9"	$9.00
Covered Dish	$40.00	Sauce Boat	$18.00
Cream	$13.00	Sauce Boat (Fast Stand)	$24.50
Dish (Platter), 11"	$16.00	Sauce Boat Stand	$10.00
Dish (Platter), 13"	$22.00	Sugar, covered	$18.00
Dish (Platter), 15"	$26.00	Teacup (only)	$5.00
Dish (Platter), 17"	$28.00	Teacup Saucer (only)	$3.00
Egg Cup	$17.50	Teapot	$70.00
Fruit, 5"	$5.00	Tureen	$50.00
Jug, ½ pt.	$20.00	Tureen Ladle	$25.00
Jug, 1 pt.	$25.00	Tureen Stand	$12.00
Jug, 3¼ pt.	$35.00		

OTHER GLOBE SHAPES

Plate 90: Globe 101. Covered dish and 15" dish (platter) in green and white of an unnamed Globe shape. Description of points to look for: The flatware is unevenly scalloped. The hollow ware has a scalloped foot, elaborate handles, and a finial the looks like two hands meeting. The embossing consists of beading and fancy scrolls.

Plate 91: Globe 102. Covered dish and 15" dish (platter) with blue and gold trim. Description of points to look for: Flatware of this shape is very evenly scalloped. Hollow ware has handles and finials in the shape of a flattened circle with a ball-like protrusion in the middle. The platter has no embossing, while the covered dish has very light embossing on the lid and around the handles.

Plate 92: Globe 103. Small Globe jug or creamer from the collection of Federick Morth.

The Goodwin Pottery Company can trace its lineage back to England through John Goodwin, who came to the United States in 1842. During the course of several potting enterprises centered in both East Liverpool and Trenton, he succeeded in training his sons in the art of pottery making. After he died in 1875, his sons (Henry, James, and George) founded the Goodwin Brothers Pottery Company which made Rockingham and yellow ware. After a period of remodeling, the making of yellow ware was dropped and the company began making c.c. ware. Sometime before 1891 the company began making white ware, which was called "Pearl White." Finally, in 1893 the brothers incorporated their company as the Goodwin Pottery Company. Soon after this, the making of both c.c. and "Pearl White" was abandoned, and they began making ironstone and semiporcelain. In 1913 the Goodwin family withdrew from china making, leasing their plant to another company.

Goodwin pieces are very rare on the West Coast and should be considered rare anywhere else. This is not surprising considering the short period of production and the early date at which their operation ended. The examples of Goodwin that we have found reflect an average level of workmanship for the time. It was my good fortune to hear of a lady (in her late 90s) who uses Virginia Rose for her everyday china and a set of Goodwin for her "good" china. Photos of pieces from this set are shown on the following pages.

GOODWIN POTTERY CO.
Specialty Plates......$15.00 – $25.00.

Plate 93: Goodwin 100. Cake or specialty plate found in the Ohio area. One similar was also found in the Southern California area.

Plate 94: Goodwin backstamp found on the platter and plate shown on page 56. Gates and Ormerod[1] date this mark as 1906.

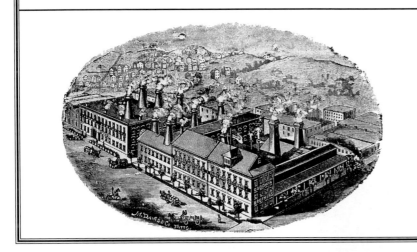

1834

The

EAST LIVERPOOL
MESSENGER

A Magazine of Good-Will

CENTENNIAL NUMBER

1934

Plate 95: The Goodwin Brothers pottery from *The East Liverpool Messenger*, dated 1934. [From the East Liverpool Museum of Ceramics.]

Plates 96, 97, 98: Goodwin 101. 13" dish (platter) of an unknown shape. This shape has a lightly scalloped edge with four indentations spaced uniformly about the rim. A close-up of the embossing is shown in Plate 97, below. Goodwin 102. 10" plate of another unidentified shape. The plate has an uneven edge. Its embossing is shown in Plate 98 at bottom right.

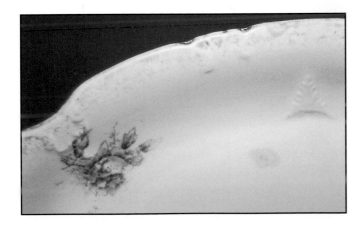

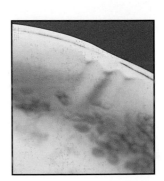

Goodwin

Baker, 8"	$11.00
Baker, 9"	$13.00
Baker, 10"	$15.00
Bone Dish	$8.00
Bowl, deep, 1 pt.	$13.00
Bowl, deep, 1½ pt.	$11.00
Butter, covered	$50.00
Butter, individual	$7.50
Casserole, covered	$35.00
Coffee Cup	$9.00
Coffee Saucer	$7.00
Coffee Saucer, AD	$10.00
Coffee, AD	$15.00
Covered Dish	$30.00
Creamer	$12.00
Dish (Platter), 11"	$14.00
Dish (Platter), 13"	$18.00
Dish (Platter), 15"	$22.00
Dish (Platter), 17"	$25.00
Egg Cup	$17.50
Fruit, 5"	$4.00
Jug, ½ pt.	$15.00
Jug, 1 pt.	$25.00
Jug, 3¼ pt.	$35.00
Jug, 5 pt.	$40.00
Nappy, 8"	$16.00
Nappy, 9"	$18.00
Nappy, 10"	$20.00
Oatmeal, 6"	$7.00
Pickle	$14.00
Plate (Coupe Soup), 8"	$8.00
Plate, 6"	$4.50
Plate, 7"	$5.50
Plate, 8"	$7.00
Plate, 9"	$9.00
Plate, 10"	$10.00
Plate, deep (Rim Soup), 9"	$8.00
Sauce Boat	$18.00
Sauce Boat (Fast Stand)	$22.50
Sauce Boat Stand	$9.00
Sugar, Covered	$18.00
Teacup (only)	$5.00
Teacup Saucer (only)	$3.00
Teapot	$70.00
Tureen	$50.00
Tureen Ladle	$25.00
Tureen Stand	$12.00

Except for a catalog of their Rockingham wares, I have yet to find any catalogs showing Goodwin wares and providing their names for their different shapes.

Plate 99: Goodwin 102. Shown are the casserole, relish, butter dish, and sugar covered with purple, white, and yellow flowers.

Another unidentified shape that has embossing that looks like a lady with a full skirt being twirled about (see the butter dish, casserole, and sugar in Plate 99). The finials can best be seen on the butter and sugar in Plate 99, as can the handles on the sugar and sauce boat. Something else that catches the eye is the scalloped, pronounced foot on such pieces as the sauce boat and casserole. The flatware is lightly embossed and has an irregular scalloped look. The pieces in Plates 99 and 100 are from a set owned by a lady who passed away in her 99th year leaving them to a collector whom she knew would treasure them as she had.

Plate 100: Goodwin 102. Saucer and sauce boat.

Plate 101: Goodwin 103. Creamer and sugar with small blue flowers and brown leaves from the collection of Frederick Morth.

The Homer Laughlin China Company

The Homer Laughlin China Company was founded in 1871, when Homer Laughlin and his brother Shakespeare built a small pottery in East Liverpool, Ohio. In the following year the city fathers of East Liverpool put up a prize of $5,000 to induce a potter to establish a plant for making white ware, a much more elegant type of china than the yellow ware made from the local clays. Homer and his brother claimed this prize when they established a two-kiln pottery for making semivitreous china.

By the fall of 1874, the company was known as the Ohio Valley Pottery, employing over 100 workers. Two years later in 1876, the company received the highest award at the Centennial Exposition in Philadelphia for their white ware. This established HLC as a pottery finally able to challenge the quality and elegance of the British china that was then being imported into America. The Homer Laughlin backstamps from this period make no secret of these aspirations, in that many of them incorporate a picture of the American eagle attacking the British lion which is lying on its back.

In 1897 Homer Laughlin, having already bought out his brother's share of the business some years before in 1877, sold out completely to a group headed by Mr. W.E. Wells, who took over responsibility for the operation of the HLC plant, and Louis I. Aaron and his sons Marcus Aaron and Charles I. Aaron. Mr. Louis Aaron assumed responsibility for the presidency of the company and for its financial affairs. Under the guidance of Mr. Wells as general manager and Mr. Aaron as president the company prospered, becoming in time the largest pottery in the world. These positions continue to be held by the Wells and Aaron families respectively, until the present day.

During its prolonged history the company employed several important technical and artistic contributors, including Dr. Albert Bleininger, a noted ceramics engineer who joined the company in 1920, and Mr. Frederick Rhead, who joined the company in 1927 as art director. Mr. Rhead was succeeded after his death in the 1940s by Mr. Don Schreckengost. These men and their colleagues were responsible for the innovative glazes and designs that emerged from HLC during the 1930s, 1940s, and 1950s. They brought us the highly-prized Fiesta as well as the delicate Eggshell shapes. The Homer Laughlin China Company is still very much alive and well today, occupying extensive facilities in Newell, West Virginia, just across the Ohio River from East Liverpool where they began.

Today Homer Laughlin china from the period covered by this book is readily found in antiques stores and flea markets, although the older shapes tend to be quite rare. The newer shapes such as Hudson, Angelus, and Genesee can be found in an afternoon. To go further back, to shapes like Louis XVI and Rococo, requires much greater effort. Nevertheless, we are privileged to own examples of both of these old shapes. Still earlier names like Victor and the legendary Shakespeare are rarely seen but do exist; your next visit to an out-of-the-way shop in a small town could turn up yet another piece.

Plate 102: The Homer Laughlin pottery at the East Liverpool site.

Plate 103: Molasses can with a metal lid from around 1900. [From the collection of Chip Simpson and Jeanie Milburn.]

VICTOR

Victor is one of the very earliest Homer Laughlin shapes. A picture from the *Crockery and Glass Journal* in Minnie Watson Kamm's book *Old China* is dated 1884. Once I shared this picture with other HLC collectors some pieces of Victor started showing up. Victor today is quite rare, this being undoubtedly due to its age and the fact that when it was produced the HLC plant was simply not able to make that much china.

Description of what to look for: The Victor shape is unusual for the time of its production in that it does not sport the extremely elaborate embossing. Instead, Victor presents a no nonsense, massive, and highly functional appearance. Decorative embossing is, for the most part, restricted to the handles and finials. The Victor finial, seen best on the teapot on page 62, is a dead give-away. It consists of a short, vertical slab with fan-shaped embossing in the center and a scroll-like support on either side. The handles, particularly of the teapot and jug, are simple in shape and easy to grasp. The handle is lightly embossed with a pattern resembling a bundle of straw, bound at the corners of the handle. Not surprisingly, it is referred to in the *Crockery and Glass Journal* as "serviceable." The backstamp reads: Premium White Stone China. It was still being sold in 1890 because it, along with the Shakespeare shape, is mentioned in the *Crockery and Glass Journal* published in that year.

I found a Victor teapot in Santa Barbara, California, which had been sadly mutilated. Somewhere along the line one of the small tabs on the side of the finial had become broken. The antiques dealer (or perhaps someone else) had carefully ground off the opposing tab, so that the finial looked almost like it was meant to be that way. In spite of this unauthorized modification, the Victor outline was easily recognizable. This teapot, the only piece of Victor that I own, today sits proudly on my shelf in spite of its wounded appearance.

For pricing see Rococo value guide on page 69.

Plate 104: Victor backstamp.

Plate 105: Victor 100. Tureen and ladle from the collection of Judi Wilfong, Buffalo, Texas.

Plate 106: Victor 101. Teapot with the Moss Rose decoration, which was a favorite of those times and was used by many potteries. The transfer decoration on this piece is exceptionally well executed. The outline of the design was first produced on paper in a brown tone, then transferred to the piece to be decorated. Other colors were then painted on: the stems and leaves in greens, the roses in pink-red, and smaller flowers in an almost cobalt blue.

SHAKESPEARE

I first learned of this elusive shape during research efforts for my book on Homer Laughlin dinnerware. I managed to locate a small book called *Old China* published privately by Minnie Kamm[4] in the 1950s. There in its pages was a reproduction of an old advertisement by Homer Laughlin showing the Shakespeare shape. This shape, undoubtedly named for Homer's brother Shakespeare, presented an odd appearance. The lids of pieces like the casserole appeared concave in the center, like someone had pressed down on the wet clay immediately after the piece was molded. I attributed this appearance to the hand of the artist who drew the advertisement, since these illustrations often look like the artist had never seen a piece of dinnerware. Never did I expect to see a piece of Shakespeare, since it was made over 100 years ago during the early days of the pottery.

In 1994, while attending the East Liverpool Collector's Convention, I encountered an unidentified Homer Laughlin sauce boat in the unexhibited collection of the Museum of Ceramics which I photographed for later reference. A couple of days later, while touring the Thompson House in East Liverpool, I saw a sauce tureen which was on display with the same depressed lid as shown in the old advertisement! I looked carefully, and indeed, I had found the Shakespeare shape. Looking back at the sauce boat I had photographed, I could see the same characteristic embossing as was seen on the tureen. It, too, was Shakespeare.

The most recent episode in the quest for Shakespeare took place in the spring of 1995, when a friend of mine found and purchased a set of Shakespeare at a dinnerware show. She graciously provided me with several pieces including a dinner plate, a cup, and a saucer. Not only had I seen Shakespeare, I now even owned some pieces of it.

Pieces of Shakespeare can be recognized in several ways. If it is a piece of lidded hollow ware, the depressed center of the lid will give it away in an instant. The embossing on the handles of pieces like the tureen and sauce boat pictured presents an accordion-like appearance. The flatware also presents some unusual features. Saucers, for example, are the deepest I've ever seen. A careful examination of this piece makes it questionable whether it belongs under the teacup with which it is shown. More likely, a larger coffee cup once sat upon it. The flatware that I've seen is quite simple in design, being utterly devoid of embossing of any sort. The pieces all carry the early eagle and lion backstamp.

For pricing, use Rococo value guide on page 69 and price 25% higher.

Plate 107· Backstamp from the Shakespeare sauce boat shown in Plate 108.

Plate 108: Creamer, sauce tureen, cup, and saucer. [Photo from Leota Bonhert.]

Plate 109: Sauce boat. [From the collection at the East Liverpool Museum of Ceramics.]

LOUIS XVI

This very old and singular shape turned up in a most unusual way. I received a phone call from a gentleman who was researching the genealogy of his family. He was trying to trace information about some dishes that had belonged to his grandparents. Although his china bore a Homer Laughlin mark, his description of these dishes, shown in Plate 110, did not correspond to any Homer Laughlin china I had ever heard of. He had photos taken and sent them to me. The leaf-like design on the flatware is recessed, and would be more appropriately called intaglio than embossing. I was amazed to see handles on the hollow ware that looked like tusks.

Here is information gleamed from the *Crockery & Glass Journal* of June 5, 1890, and sent to me by Richard Daurghty of Romeo, IL, who is the owner of the set of Louis XVI:

"Homer Laughlin has his new dinner service now in the warehouse ready for the market. It has been named Louis XVI, and I think very appropriately. The entire service carries raised clay scroll lines — the same ornamentation appearing on every piece in the set. While sample sets can now be forwarded, it will not be in stock for custom shipment before July 1st. Mr. Laughlin has had carved out five new designs in ornamentation for the Louis XVI, which are entirely new in conception and execution — totally different from anything seen in this country. One of the characteristics of the decoration Mr. Laughlin has applied to this fine grade of stone porcelain is a combination of effective ground shadows and panels traced in geometrical outline and graceful curves in and around the raised clay treatment secured in modeling. These ground shadow coloring are new art effects in ceramic burning and one is a delicate "cafe au lait," while another is a light tinted ivory shading. The modeling of the handles is a treatment of a curled tusk, over which is a color wash of burnt ivory. The gliding is an embellishment introduced specially to emphasize the modeling and show out its best beauty in graceful flowing curves. Mr. Laughlin has made some special pieces in this elegant style not a part of the regular dinner set, but which go with it as companion pieces. These new novelties in ceramic art are chocolate pots, boufe[sic] jugs and orange bowls. The decoration on these special pieces are weird yet beautiful effects secured through mat coloring of odd new tints on mat grounds or under shadows."

For pricing use Rococo value guide on page 69 and price 50% higher.

Plate 110: Louis XIV 100. Dishes (platters), dinner plate, sauce boat, and individual butter. [From the collection of Richard Daurghty.]

Plate 111: Louis XIV 101. Covered dish. When Bill Gray, a collector and dealer in early American dinnerware, asked if I were interested in an unusual piece of Homer Laughlin that he had found, I little suspected it would be an exquisite piece of Louis XVI matching those of Richard Daurghty.

ROCOCO

For several years I've had a copy of an 1896 Homer Laughlin catalog showing Rococo jugs, as well as an advertisement by an HLC distributor showing a Rococo casserole and plate. It was not until my last trip to the Homer Laughlin factory that an 1895 Rococo catalog was located and I was able to see the full extent of the pieces included in this shape.

Description of what to look for: The theme of the Rococo shape is that of rounded cubes and rectangles. Flatware pieces will have sides that are nearly straight, connected by smoothly rounded corners. The corners will show a slight scalloped effect. Hollow ware pieces will have a firm, squat appearance. These pieces will definitely stay where they are put, with no threat of upset. The otherwise smooth sides of the hollow ware are decorated with raised, curved ridges, which suggest that the sides are not flat at all, but properly rounded. Handles are large simple curves with an embossed scroll at the top, and a sort of fan-shaped lower end. Finials are simple, asymmetrical loops embossed with tiny lines. Rococo shares some similarities with the HLC Louis XVI shape, the sauce boat and covered dish (see Plate 110 on page 66) being identical in appearance except for the embossing and handles.

Value guide on page 69.

Plate 112: Rococo 100, 15" dish (platter) and Rococo 101, large sugar bowl. The platter is decorated with a transfer of brown with painted small blue flowers. The sugar also uses a brown transfer with pink flowers and green leaves painted in.

Plate 113: Rococo 102. Teapot, the style of decoration used on this piece of Rococo was a transfer of brown morning glories.

Plate 114: Rococo 103. Butter dish from the collection of Judy Wilfong, Buffalo, Texas.

Rococo

Baker, 6"	$10.00	Jug, 5½ pt.	$45.00
Baker, 8"	$16.00	Jug, 8 pt.	$65.00
Baker, 9"	$20.00	Nappy, 4"	$12.00
Baker, 10"	$22.00	Nappy, 5"	$14.00
Bone Dish	$9.00	Nappy, 6"	$16.00
Bowl, deep, 1 pt.	$12.00	Nappy, 7"	$18.00
Bowl, deep, 1½ pt.	$14.00	Nappy, 8"	$20.00
Bowl, oyster, 1 pt.	$13.00	Nappy, 9"	$24.00
Bowl, oyster, 1½ pt.	$15.00	Nappy, 10"	$26.00
Butter, covered	$55.00	Newport, 7"	$30.00
Butter, individual	$5.50	Newport, 8"	$40.00
Cake Plate	$25.00	Newport, 9"	$45.00
Casserole, covered, 8"	$45.00	Oatmeal, 6"	$8.00
Casserole, covered, 9"	$50.00	Pickle, Oak, Grape Leaf	$32.00
Coffee Cup	$12.00	Plate (Coupe Soup), 8"	$8.00
Coffee Saucer	$7.00	Plate, 6"	$5.50
Coffee Saucer, AD	$8.00	Plate, 7"	$7.00
Coffee Cup, AD	$18.00	Plate, 8"	$8.50
Comport	$65.00	Plate, 9"	$10.00
Covered Dish, 8"	$45.00	Plate, 10"	$12.00
Covered Dish, 9"	$40.00	Plate, deep (Rim Soup), 8"	$8.00
Cream, 42s (small)	$12.00	Plate, deep (Rim Soup), 9"	$9.00
Cream, 36s (med.)	$14.00	Sauce Boat	$18.00
Cream, 30s (large)	$16.00	Sauce Ladle	$22.00
Dish (Platter), 8"	$14.00	Sauce Tureen Stand	$12.50
Dish (Platter), 10"	$16.00	Sauce Tureen, 6"	$40.00
Dish (Platter), 12"	$18.00	Soup Tureen	$85.00
Dish (Platter), 14"	$22.00	Soup Tureen, Stand	$20.00
Dish (Platter), 16"	$26.00	Spoon Holder (Spooner)	$48.00
Fruit, 5"	$6.00	Sugar, covered	$24.00
Fruit, 6"	$7.00	Teacup (only)	$5.00
Jug, ¾ pt.	$20.00	Teacup Saucer (only)	$3.00
Jug, 1 pt.	$23.00	Teapot	$75.00
Jug, 1¾ pt.	$25.00	Tureen, oyster, Stand	$15.00
Jug, 2½ pt.	$30.00	Tureen, oyster, covered	$65.00
Jug, 4 pt.	$40.00		

Plate 115: Rococo backstamp.

BAKERS.

JUGS.

SALADS.

BUTTERS.

COMPORTS.

NEWPORT SALADS.

SAUCE BOATS.

OATMEALS.

SUGARS

COVERED DISHES.

PICKLES.

TEAS.

DISH.

PLATES.

Teapots

Plate 116: Catalog pictures of Rococo.

GOLDEN GATE

I first discovered the existence of this shape during a visit to the HLC plant archives in 1993. I kept finding copies of old invoices describing the shipment of something called "Golden Gate." It finally dawned on me that this was the name of another HLC shape! Of course, having found the name, it became a real challenge to see what it looked like. Friends in the Ohio area called me to say they had found a sauce boat with a Golden Gate backstamp, which they obligingly shipped to me. More pieces have since turned up in the Ohio area, and I recently found a 90-piece set in Sacramento, California. I think this early Homer Laughlin shape is a thrill to find because it is so old. It was equally a thrill to see the beautifully ornate cover of its catalog book dated 1896. Golden Gate is not plentiful, but it can be found of one is willing to search for it.

Description of points to look for: Although Golden Gate can be immediately identified by means of its backstamp, one must still recognize it as interesting in order to turn it over and look at the mark. Golden Gate flatware is identified by its special embossing about the rim, easily seen in the beautifully decorated plate in Plate 118. Hollow ware pieces such as the covered dish present a definite flattened appearance. Note the large overhang of the lid over the body of the piece. Like the Colonial shape, Golden Gate included a Geisha shape, which had a high straight-sided look in comparison to the squat, rounded shape of their standard counterparts. The differences between the standard and the Geisha shapes can be easily seen in Plates 121 and 122. Like Colonial, this shape also lists several exotic pieces such as newports, which are squarc nappys and a toast rack.

Plate 117: Golden Gate backstamp.

Plate 118: Golden Gate 100. 10" plate that was found and photographed at the East Liverpool Museum of Ceramics. I found it on a shelf in storage and was astonished by its beauty.

Plate 119: Golden Gate 101. This covered dish has a cobalt blue design.

Plate 120: Golden Gate 102. Butter dish with a beautiful violet colored transfer decoration featuring a cottage by a lake.

Plate 121: Golden Gate 102. This creamer matches the butter dish in Plate 120. [From the collection of Brenda Wood.]

Plate 122: Golden Gate 103. A Golden Gate creamer in the Geisha shape. Contrast its shape with that of the standard Golden Gate creamer in the previous illustration. The backstamps on both pieces say "Golden Gate." [Both this piece and the butter dish in Plate 120 are from the collection of Judi Wilfong.]

Plate 123: Golden Gate 104. An oyster bowl decorated beautifully with large green leaves, possibly hand painted.

Plate 124: Golden Gate 105. 10" plate, cup, saucer, and individual butter.

Plate 125: Golden Gate 105. 13" platter, 9" newport, cup, and saucer.

GOLDEN GATE

Baker, 5½"	$12.00	Jug, 5½ pt.	$45.00
Baker, 7"	$20.00	Jug, 8 pt.	$65.00
Baker, 8"	$22.00	Jug, Geisha (small)	$25.00
Baker, 9"	$24.00	Jug, Geisha (small-med.)	$35.00
Baker, 10"	$26.00	Jug, Geisha (medium)	$40.00
Baker, 11"	$28.00	Jug, Geisha (large)	$55.00
Bone Dish	$8.00	Jug, Geisha (ex-large)	$75.00
Bowl, deep, 1 pt.	$15.00	Nappy, 7"	$20.00
Butter, covered	$55.00	Nappy, 8"	$22.00
Butter, individual	$6.50	Nappy, 9"	$24.00
Cake Plate	$25.00	Nappy, 10"	$26.00
Casserole, covered, 8"	$45.00	Newport, 8½"	$38.00
Casserole, covered, 9"	$50.00	Newport, 9½"	$40.00
Celery Tray, 11"	$24.00	Newport, 10"	$45.00
Chop Plate, 14"	$30.00	Nut Dish	$30.00
Coffee Cup	$10.00	Oatmeal, 6"	$7.00
Coffee Saucer	$6.00	Olive, 8"	$22.00
Coffee Saucer, AD	$6.00	Pickle (handles), 8"	$25.00
Coffee, AD	$16.00	Plate (Coupe Soup), 8"	$8.00
Comportier	$95.00	Plate (Coupe Soup), 9"	$9.00
Covered Dish, 9½"	$45.00	Plate, 6"	$6.00
Covered Dish, 10"	$50.00	Plate, 7"	$7.50
Cream	$14.00	Plate, 8"	$8.50
Cream, individual	$12.00	Plate, 9"	$10.00
Custard, handled	$16.00	Plate, 10"	$12.00
Dish (Platter), 7"	$13.00	Plate, deep (Rim Soup), 9"	$9.00
Dish (Platter), 10"	$14.00	Sauce Boat	$22.00
Dish (Platter), 11"	$15.00	Sauce Boat Stand	$10.00
Dish (Platter), 12"	$18.00	Sauce Ladle	$24.00
Dish (Platter), 13"	$20.00	Sauce Tureen Stand	$12.50
Dish (Platter), 14"	$22.00	Sauce Tureen, 6"	$40.00
Dish (Platter), 15"	$23.50	Soup Ladle	$30.00
Dish (Platter), 16"	$25.00	Spoon Holder (Spooner)	$48.00
Dish (Platter), 17"	$30.00	Sugar, covered	$24.00
Dish (Platter), 19"	$35.00	Sugar, Geisha	$20.00
Egg Cup	$17.50	Sugar, individual	$16.00
Fancy Slaw, 10"	$40.00	Teacup (only)	$6.00
Fancy Slaw, 11"	$42.00	Teacup Saucer (only)	$3.50
Fancy Slaw, 12"	$45.00	Teapot	$75.00
Fruit, 5"	$5.00	Teapot, Geisha	$90.00
Fruit, 6"	$7.00	Teapot, individual	$45.00
Jug, ¾ pt.	$20.00	Toast Rack	$95.00
Jug, 1 pt.	$22.00	Tureen Stand	$15.00
Jug, 1 pt.	$25.00	Tureen, Soup	$85.00
Jug, 2½ pt.	$30.00	Tureen, oyster	$65.00
Jug, 4 pt.	$35.00		

Plates 126: Catalog picture of Golden Gate.

1 Covered Dish	8 Soup Tureen	15 Teapot	22 Bone Dish
2 Sauce Tureen	9 Covered Butter	16 Sugar	23 Coffee
3 Casserole	10 Coupe Soup	17 Plate, deep (Rim Soup)	24 Tea
4 Fancy Slaw	11 Plate, 6"	18 Plate 10"	25 A.D. Coffee
5 Cake Plate	12 Spooner	19 Plate, 9"	26 Egg Cup
6 Dish (Platter)	13 Creamer	20 Plate, 8"	27 Bowl
7 Oyster Tureen	14 Butter, individual	21 Plate, 7"	

Plates 127: Catalog picture of Golden Gate.

AMERICAN BEAUTY

This shape, found in the same 1899 HLC catalog as Golden Gate, offers many of the same unusual pieces. This shape probably consisted of more individual items than any other HLC line. Purchasers could choose from over 90 individual pieces, including platters ranging in size from 6" to 19", five different sizes of bakers, three different newports (square serving bowls), plus a range of unusual items such as dishes for serving olives and pickles, and a toast rack.

American Beauty is shown in the 1908 Sears, Roebuck & Co. catalog and was sold through Sears and other mail-order outlets. American Beauty is not as readily found as some of the later HLC shapes, possibly due to a more limited production lifetime. Nevertheless, American Beauty can still be found often enough in today's antiques markets to reward the collector.

I recently came across three bone dishes being sold together in a Southern California antiques store. The three were identical, all white with no decals; however, the embossing on each was much different in definition. One was very well defined, the second less so, and on the third the embossing was very difficult to make out. Turning them over I discovered three different American Beauty backstamps.

Plates 128, 129, and 130: Three American Beauty backstamps.

Plate 131: American Beauty 100. 18" dish (platter).

Plate 132: American Beauty 101. Listed as a celery tray, this beautiful piece seems like it would be a better decoration on the wall or the table of a formal room. This piece was found on a back room shelf at the East Liverpool Museum of Ceramics.

Plate 133: American Beauty 102. It was a thrill when Bill Gray of Maryland called to offer me this unusual piece of American Beauty. It is listed as a comportier (look up its function on page 248). This wonderful piece was a causality of the Jan. 17, 1994, Northridge earthquake. However, the pieces have been saved so that it can be restored.

Plate 134: American Beauty 103. The handles and finial on this sugar bowl show the American Beauty family resemblance in both their shape and placement. Contrast this sugar with the individual sugar, whose handles more closely resemble those of the spooner shown in the 1896 HLC catalog on page 81. [From the Judi Wilfong collection.]

Plate 135: American Beauty 104. Creamer, casserole, and bone dish.

AMERICAN BEAUTY

Baker, 5½"...$10.00	Fruit, 5"...$5.00
Baker, 8" $16.00	Fruit, 6"..$7.00
Baker, 9" $18.00	Jug, ¾ pt. $18.00
Baker, 10" $22.00	Jug, 1 pt. $22.00
Baker, 11" $26.00	Jug, 1¾ pt. $25.00
Bone Dish...$8.00	Jug, 2½ pt. $30.00
Bowl, deep, 1 pt. $12.00	Jug, 4 pt. $35.00
Bowl, deep, 1½ pt...........................$13.00	Jug, 5½ pt. $40.00
Bowl, oyster, 1 pt. $10.00	Jug, 8 pt. $55.00
Bowl, oyster, 1½ pt. $11.00	Ladle $22.00
Bowl, oyster, 2 pt. $14.00	Nappy, 7"...$12.00
Butter, covered $50.00	Nappy, 8"...$16.00
Butter, individual $6.50	Nappy, 9"...$20.00
Cake Plate $25.00	Nappy, 10"..$24.00
Casserole, covered, 8" $45.00	Newport, 8½".......................................$35.00
Casserole, covered, 9" $50.00	Newport, 9½".......................................$40.00
Celery Tray, 11"................................$24.00	Newport, 10".......................................$45.00
Chop Plate, 14" $30.00	Oatmeal, 6½"...$8.00
Coffee Cup..$12.00	Olive, 8"..$20.00
Coffee Saucer $7.00	Pickle (handle), 8"..............................$25.00
Coffee Saucer, AD............................$10.00	Plate (Coupe Soup), 8" $8.00
Coffee, AD $15.00	Plate (Coupe Soup), 9" $9.00
Comportier $95.00	Plate, 6" $4.50
Covered Dish, 9½".............................$40.00	Plate, 7" $5.50
Covered Dish, 10".............................$45.00	Plate, 8" $8.50
Cream..$12.00	Plate, 9" $9.00
Cream Soup $15.00	Plate, 10" $10.00
Cream Soup Stand $8.00	Plate, deep (Rim Soup), 9"...................$9.00
Cream, individual..............................$10.00	Sauce Boat $18.00
Custard, handled $15.00	Sauce Boat Stand $9.00
Dish (Platter), 6"..............................$10.00	Sauce Ladle..$22.00
Dish (Platter), 7" $11.00	Sauce Tureen Stand $12.50
Dish (Platter), 8" $12.00	Sauce Tureen, 6"................................$35.00
Dish (Platter), 9" $14.00	Soup Ladle $25.00
Dish (Platter), 10" $16.00	Spoon Holder (Spooner) $52.00
Dish (Platter), 12" $18.00	Sugar, covered, 1 pt............................$18.00
Dish (Platter), 13" $20.50	Sugar, covered, 1½ pt. $20.00
Dish (Platter), 14" $22.00	Sugar, individual................................$14.00
Dish (Platter), 15" $24.00	Teacup (only).......................................$5.00
Dish (Platter), 16" $26.00	Teacup Saucer (only) $3.00
Dish (Platter), 17" $28.00	Teapot $70.00
Dish (Platter), 18" $30.00	Toast Rack..$95.00
Dish (Platter), 19" $32.00	Tureen Stand $19.00
Egg Cup...$17.50	Tureen, Soup $70.00
Fruit Bowl $45.00	Tureen, oyster.....................................$40.00

Plate 136: Catalog picture of American Beauty.

1 Sauce Boat	11 Tea	20 Bowl	29 Plate
2 Toast Rack	12 Coffee	21 Oyster Bowl	30 Cake
3 Egg Cup	13 Pickle	22 Oatmeal	31 Deep Plate
4 Sugar	14 Celery Tray	23 Comportier	32 Dish
5 Teapot	15 Olive	24 Coupe Soup	33 Oyster Tureen
6 Cream	16 Fruit	25 Nappy	34 Casserole
7 Custard	17 Individual Butter	26 Baker	35 Sauce Tureen Complete
8 Spooner	18 Bone	27 Covered Dish	36 Fruit Bowl
9 Jugs	19 Covered Butter	28 Chop Plate	37 Soup Tureen Complete
10 A.D. Coffee			

SENECA

Seneca made its appearance somewhere around 1901, appearing in Sears Roebuck & Co. catalogs from that period. The pattern seen most often in the catalogs is called "Our Green and Holly dinner set" which features red holly berries and green holly leaves. There is also an advertisement in a 1906 Sears catalog which features the "American Beauty" dinner set. A detailed examination of the pieces pictured in the ad, particularly the jug and the covered dish, reveals that this is really the Seneca shape, probably with a decoration called "American Beauty." The availability of Seneca is typical for 95 year old American dinnerware (i.e., scarce). There is probably more of it than appears, since pieces of the Seneca shape can often be positively identified only through the general shape of the piece because the backstamp is most often seen without the Seneca name. (See page 83 for backstamps).

Plate 137: Seneca 100 (right). This Seneca jug with its decal of a young woman is different in shape from the Seneca creamer next to it. The jugs all have a round smooth appearance with a rounded ridge in the mold at the sides. Seneca 101. This Seneca creamer with its decoration of flowers appears with ridges molded in a regular pattern all the way around. It is unknown why the jugs and creamers were designed differently.

Plate 138: Seneca 102. Sauce boat at the top with a pink and white roses. Seneca 103. Sauce boat at the bottom with pink and white daisies.

Plate 139: Seneca 104. An example of the Seneca covered dish. Notice that the lid which is mostly flat rises up almost like a small volcano in the center. The finial is a twisted loop. The handles curve upward giving it a very long look. A scattering of violets, leaves, and thread-like tendrils make up the decoration. [From the collection of Richard Racheter.]

Plate 140: Seneca from a catalog at the Homer Laughlin China Company.

1 Butter, indiv.	14 Oatmeal
2 Bone Dish	15 Plate
3 Sauce Boat	16 Baker
4 Teapot	17 Plate, deep
5 Sugar, covered	18 Plate
6 Cream	19 Cake Plate
7 Jug	20 Dish (Platter)
8 Nappy	21 Casserole
9 Bowl, deep	22 Covered Dish
10 Coffee Cup	23 Butter, covered
11 Teacup	24 Sauce Tureen
12 Pickle	25 Tureen, oyster
13 Fruit	

Plate 141: Backstamp with the Seneca name in it.

Plate 142: Backstamp most often found on Seneca. Note the words: "white granite" in the backstamp. This may be another key to locating Seneca.

SENECA

Baker, 5½"	$12.00
Baker, 7"	$15.00
Baker, 8"	$16.00
Baker, 9"	$18.00
Baker, 10"	$20.00
Bone Dish	$8.00
Bowl, deep, 1 pt.	$11.00
Bowl, deep, 1½ pt.	$13.00
Butter, covered	$50.00
Butter, individual	$5.50
Cake Plate	$25.00
Casserole, covered, 8"	$40.00
Casserole, covered, 9"	$45.00
Celery Tray, 11"	$20.00
Chop Plate, 14"	$30.00
Coffee Cup	$12.00
Coffee Saucer	$7.00
Coffee Saucer, AD	$16.00
Coffee, AD	$14.00
Comportier	$75.00
Covered Dish, 9½"	$35.00
Covered Dish, 10"	$40.00
Cream	$12.00
Cream Soup	$14.00
Cream Soup Stand	$11.00
Cream, individual	$10.00
Custard, handled	$15.00
Dish (Platter), 6"	$7.00
Dish (Platter), 7"	$8.00
Dish (Platter), 8"	$10.00
Dish (Platter), 9"	$12.00
Dish (Platter), 10"	$13.00
Dish (Platter), 12"	$14.00
Dish (Platter), 13"	$15.50
Dish (Platter), 14"	$18.00
Dish (Platter), 15"	$20.00
Dish (Platter), 16"	$22.00
Dish (Platter), 17"	$25.00
Dish (Platter), 19"	$30.00
Egg Cup	$17.50
Fruit Bowl	$45.00
Fruit, 5"	$4.00
Fruit, 6"	$7.00
Jug, ¾ pt.	$20.00
Jug, 1 pt.	$22.00
Jug, 1¾ pt.	$25.00
Jug, 2½ pt.	$30.00
Jug, 4 pt.	$35.00
Jug, 5½ pt.	$40.00
Jug, 8 pt.	$65.00
Ladle	$22.00
Nappy, 7"	$10.00
Nappy, 8"	$16.00
Nappy, 9"	$18.00
Nappy, 10"	$20.00
Oatmeal, 36	$6.00
Oatmeal, 30	$7.00
Olive, 8"	$18.00
Pickle (Handles), 8"	$20.00
Plate (Coupe Soup), 8"	$8.00
Plate (Coupe Soup), 9"	$9.00
Plate, 6"	$4.50
Plate, 7"	$5.50
Plate, 8"	$7.50
Plate, 9"	$9.00
Plate, 10"	$10.00
Plate, deep (Rim Soup), 9"	$9.00
Sauce Boat	$18.00
Sauce Boat Stand	$9.00
Sauce Ladle	$22.00
Sauce Tureen Stand	$10.50
Sauce Tureen, 6"	$35.00
Soup Ladle	$25.00
Spoon Holder (Spooner)	$42.00
Sugar, covered, 1 pt.	$18.00
Sugar, covered, 1½ pt.	$22.00
Sugar, individual	$14.00
Teacup (only)	$6.00
Teacup Saucer (only)	$3.00
Teapot	$65.00
Tureen Stand	$15.00
Tureen, covered	$55.00
Tureen, oyster	$65.00

COLONIAL

The Colonial shape dates from about 1901. Colonial is one of the most eccentrically elaborate of the Homer Laughlin shapes. Pieces have a baroque, exuberant style, typical of much of the turn-of-the-century dinnerware. Collectors should note that Colonial hollow ware (creamer, sugar, teapot, jugs) were made in two quite different styles. The standard Colonial shape was quite ornate, as seen in the top row of the catalog page in Plate 151. The Colonial Geisha shape, however, has a much simpler appearance, more like the HLC Hudson shape (see page 95).

Although the Colonial shape is not common, it was shown for many years in both the Sears, Roebuck & Co. and Montgomery Ward & Co. catalogs. It is thus found often enough to warrant interest as a collectable shape, which can be easily identified by means of its distinctive mark, shown in Plate 143. Take care also, that there may be a piece of Colonial Geisha masquerading as the more common Hudson hollow ware.

Description of points to look for: Flatware will have little to set it apart from other wares of that time. Rims of the platters and plates will have light embossing with the edges of the rims showing a slight scalloped appearance. It is in the hollow ware that Colonial shouts for attention. Jugs, sauce boats, creams and sugars, casseroles, covered dishes, and teapots all have a foot, which rises to a well defined flare, almost as though they were wearing some sort of skirt. The edges of the rims are heavily scalloped. Lids have a heavily embossed pattern about the tops, near the handles. Then there are the handles themselves: they swirl and twirl and bear all sorts of little excrescences and embossing. The lid of the covered dish shown in Plate 147 is truly a wonder to behold.

Value guide on page 88.

Plates 143, 144, and 145: Three different backstamps found on the Colonial shape.

Plate 146: Colonial 100. 13" dish (platter), creamer, sauce boat and stand, and tea cup and saucer. This set, pictured in the 1901 Sears catalog, was called "Our White and Gold Colonial pattern." Like other early ware, this set sports two distinct backstamps, shown in Plates 144 and 145. [This set is from the Richard Racheter collection.]

Plate 147: A close-up of the covered dish from the set in Plate 146.

Plate 148: Homer Laughlin Colonial Violet pattern. The sauce boat on the left is shown in the 1902 Montgomery Ward & Co. catalog. Colonial 101, sauce boat on the right with a band of pink roses. While both are marked Colonial, the sauce boat on the left, has a much less pronounced foot than the sauce boat on the right. Furthermore the one on the far left is the same as that pictured in the Homer Laughlin catalog on page 89. What is the other sauce boat? After a little digging I turned up a very early Colonial picture showing this same sauce boat with its very pronounced foot, which must have been the original sauce boat design. I believe this is another case of remodeling. [From the Judi Wilfong collection.]

Plate 149: Colonial 102. Homer Laughlin excelled in ornate pickle dishes, some bizarrely unrelated to the general design of the dinner set. This 7" feathered Colonial pickle is richly gilded, decorated with a strip of holes along one rim in imitation of an abalone shell. [From the collection of Richard Racheter.]

Plate 150: Colonial 103. This butter dish, surprisingly, has a Hudson bottom while the top is clearly Colonial. Another Homer Laughlin mystery. [From the collection of Richard Racheter.]

COLONIAL

Baker, 5"	$10.00	Jug, 30s (medium)	$40.00
Baker, 7"	$16.00	Jug, 24s (med.–Large)	$45.00
Baker, 8"	$18.00	Jug, 12s (large)	$50.00
Baker, 9"	$22.00	Jug, 6s (ex-large)	$65.00
Baker, 10"	$24.00	Jug, Geisha, 5s (small)	$20.00
Baker, 11"	$26.00	Jug, Geisha, 4s (small–med.)	$30.00
Bone Dish	$8.00	Jug, Geisha, 2s (medium)	$40.00
Bullion Cup, 6 oz.	$14.50	Jug, Geisha, 1s (large)	$50.00
Bullion Saucer	$6.00	Ladle	$22.00
Bowl, deep, 36s	$14.00	Nappy, 7"	$16.00
Bowl, deep, 30s	$16.00	Nappy, 8"	$18.00
Bowl, oyster, 36s	$10.00	Nappy, 9"	$22.00
Bowl, oyster, 30s	$12.00	Nappy, 10"	$24.00
Bowl, oyster, 24s	$14.00	Newport, 7"	$18.00
Butter, covered	$65.00	Newport, 8"	$35.00
Butter, individual	$6.50	Newport, 9"	$40.00
Cake Plate	$28.00	Newport, 10"	$45.00
Celery Tray	$28.00	Oatmeal	$8.00
Casserole, covered, 8"	$40.00	Olive	$22.00
Casserole, covered, 9"	$45.00	Pickle	$26.00
Chop Plate	$25.00	Plate (Coupe Soup), 7"	$8.00
Coffee Cup	$10.00	Plate (Coupe Soup), 8"	$9.00
Coffee Saucer	$6.00	Plate, 6"	$5.50
Coffee Saucer, AD	$6.00	Plate, 7"	$6.50
Coffee, AD	$16.00	Plate, 8"	$9.50
Covered Dish, 8"	$35.00	Plate, 9"	$9.00
Covered Dish, 9"	$40.00	Plate, 10"	$11.00
Cream	$13.00	Plate, deep (Rim Soup), 8"	$8.00
Custard	$16.00	Plate, deep (Rim Soup), 9"	$9.00
Dish (Platter), 6"	$8.00	Sauce Boat	$18.00
Dish (Platter), 7"	$10.00	Sauce Boat Stand	$9.00
Dish (Platter), 8"	$11.00	Sauce Ladle	$22.00
Dish (Platter), 9"	$14.00	Sauce Tureen Stand	$10.50
Dish (Platter), 10"	$16.00	Sauce Tureen	$35.00
Dish (Platter), 11"	$18.00	Soup Tureen	$65.00
Dish (Platter), 12"	$20.00	Soup Stand	$15.00
Dish (Platter), 13"	$22.00	Soup Ladle	$25.00
Dish (Platter), 14"	$24.00	Spoon Holder	$48.00
Dish (Platter), 15"	$26.00	Sugar, covered	$18.00
Dish (Platter), 17"	$30.00	Sugar, individual	$14.00
Egg Cup, Graham	$17.50	Teacup (only)	$6.00
Fruit, 5"	$5.00	Teacup Saucer (only)	$3.50
Fruit, 6"	$7.00	Teapot	$75.00
Fruit Bowl	$75.00	Teapot Stand	$20.00
Jug, 48s (ex-small)	$18.00	Teapots, Geisha	$85.00
Jug, 42s (small)	$22.00	Sugar, Geisha	$22.00
Jug, 36s (small–med.)	$30.00	Cream, Geisha	$16.00

Plate 151: Catalog picture of Colonial.

1	Sugar, individual	15	Spooner	29	Bowl, deep
2	Teapot, individual	16	Geisha Sugar	30	Butter, covered
3	Cream, individual	17	Geisha Teapot	31	Alaska Ice Cream
4	A.D. Coffee & Saucer	18	Geisha Cream	32	Cake Plate
5	Sugar	19	Geisha Jug	33	Dish (Platter)
6	Teapot	20	Nappy	34	Plate
7	Cream	21	Baker	35	Chop Plate
8	Jug	22	Oatmeal	36	Newport
9	Sauce Boat	23	Golden Gate Teacup & Saucer	37	Oyster Tureen
10	Pickle	24	Ovide Teacup & Saucer	38	Casserole
11	Coupe Soup	25	Rococo Teacup & Saucer	39	Sauce Tureen, complete
12	Fruit	26	Colonial Coffee & Saucer	40	Covered Dish
13	Butter, individual	27	Colonial Teacup & Saucer	41	Soup Tureen, complete
14	Egg Cup	28	Bouillon Cup & Saucer		

KING CHARLES

The King Charles shape appears in the Sears catalog of 1906. Although it shared the pages of the Sears catalog with other, better-known HLC shapes, King Charles does not appear to have been especially popular, if one is to judge popularity by the number of pieces appearing in today's antiques market. King Charles is, in fact, quite rare. When I first began work on this book in 1993, I owned not a piece of it, and knew of only two other pieces in the hands of collectors. Since that time I have been fortunate to have acquired both the lovely covered dish shown in Plate 152 and a pickle dish.

Description of points to look for: Although the flatware does not appear to have any features to set it apart, the same cannot be said for the hollow ware. The King Charles hollow ware can only be described as elegant. The first feature of King Charles that catches the eye is the pronounced foot. While many shapes from this period have prominent feet, King Charles pieces have feet that seem almost separate from the body of the piece itself. Finials are all simple loop shapes without excessive encrustations of embossing. The handles of the jug, creams, sugars, and teapot are ear-shaped with a small nub near the top. The hollow ware pieces I have examined all show delicate embossed patterns on their otherwise flat surfaces. While I have never set eyes on the flatware, I would expect to find these embossed about the rims in an equally tasteful manner.

Value guide page 92.

Plate 152: King Charles 100. Casserole with garlands of delicate pink and white flowers. Gold outlines the embossing around the finial and handles.

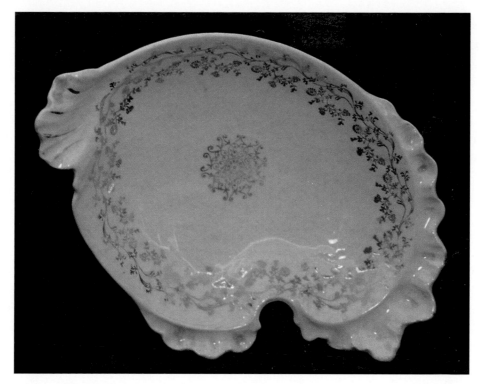

Plate 153: Arbutus pattern. This 9" pickle reminds me of an abalone shell with an extended mantle. The same motif appears in the pickle dishes of many other HLC lines from the same period. [From the collection of Richard Racheter.]

Plate 154: Arbutus pattern. A sauce boat in the King Charles shape from the collection of Judi Wilfong in Texas, has the same decoration as the pickle shown above.

KING CHARLES

Baker, 5"	$12.00	Dish (Platter), 15"	$26.00
Baker, 6"	$14.00	Dish (Platter), 16"	$28.00
Baker, 7"	$16.00	Dish (Platter), 17"	$30.00
Baker, 8"	$18.00	Dish (Platter), 18"	$32.00
Baker, 9"	$20.00	Fruit, 5"	$6.00
Baker, 10"	$24.00	Fruit, 5½"	$7.00
Baker, 11"	$28.00	Horse Radishes	$15.00
Bone Dish	$8.00	Jug, 42s (ex-small)	$20.00
Bullion Cup	$14.00	Jug, 36s (small)	$25.00
Bullion Saucer	$6.00	Jug, 30s (small–med.)	$30.00
Bowl, deep, 36s	$13.00	Jug, 24s (medium)	$35.00
Bowl, deep, 30s	$15.00	Jug, 12s (large)	$55.00
Bowl, oyster, 36s	$10.00	Jug, 6s (ex-large)	$65.00
Bowl, oyster, 30s	$14.00	Nappy, 7"	$16.00
Butter, covered	$75.00	Nappy, 8"	$18.00
Cake Plate	$25.00	Nappy, 9"	$20.00
Casserole, covered, 8"	$55.00	Nappy, 10"	$24.00
Casserole, covered, 9"	$65.00	Pickle	$25.00
Chocolate Cup	$14.00	Plate (Coupe Soup), 9"	$9.00
Chocolate Pot	$125.00	Plate, 6"	$6.00
Chocolate Saucer	$6.00	Plate, 7"	$7.00
Coffee Cup	$12.00	Plate, 8"	$8.50
Coffee Saucer	$6.00	Plate, 9"	$10.00
Coffee Saucer, AD	$6.00	Plate, 10"	$12.00
Coffee, Cup AD	$14.00	Plate, deep (Rim Soup), 9"	$10.00
Covered Dish, 8"	$45.00	Salt, Individual	$25.00
Covered Dish, 9"	$50.00	Sauce Boat	$20.00
Creamer	$16.00	Sauce Ladle	$25.00
Creamer, individual	$14.00	Sauce Tureen Stand	$12.00
Dish (Platter), 5"	$8.00	Sauce Tureen	$40.00
Dish (Platter), 6"	$9.00	Soup Ladle	$28.00
Dish (Platter), 7"	$10.00	Spoon Holder (Spooner)	$50.00
Dish (Platter), 8"	$11.00	Sugar, covered	$18.00
Dish (Platter), 9"	$12.00	Sugar, individual	$16.00
Dish (Platter), 10"	$14.00	Teacup (only)	$6.00
Dish (Platter), 11"	$16.00	Teacup Saucer (only)	$3.50
Dish (Platter), 12"	$18.00	Teapot	$85.00
Dish (Platter), 13"	$20.00	Tureen, oyster	$85.00
Dish (Platter), 14"	$22.00	Tureen, soup	$95.00

Plate 155: Catalog picture of King Charles.

1 Chocolate Pot	10 Coffee	20 Individual Salt	29 Oyster Tureen
2 Spooner	12 Tea	21 Sauce Boat	30 Casserole
3 Sugar	13 A.D. Coffee	22 Oatmeal	31 Covered Dish
4 Teapot	14 Coupe Soup	23 Baker	32 Soup Tureen
5 Cream	15 Nappy	24 Deep Plate	33 Comport
6 Mustard	16 Bone	25 Covered Butter	
7 Jug	17 Bowl	26 Plate, 7"	
8 Sauce Tureen	18 Fruit & Individual Butter	27 Cake	
9 Pickle	19 Chocolate	28 Dish	

Plate 156: King Charles backstamp.

Plate 157: King Charles backstamp.

HUDSON

The ornate Hudson shape was marketed from approximately 1906 until the late 1920s, and the potential purchaser could build a set from a selection of 68 offered pieces. Hudson is probably the easiest of the early Homer Laughlin shapes to find, either separately or in sets. This is reasonable in light of its long production run and frequent appearance in vendor catalogs. In the 1918 Sears, Roebuck & Co. catalog five different patterned sets were offered for sale.

The wide assortment of pieces hints at a substantial table arrangement, 11 sizes of dishes (platters), 8 jugs with varied capacities, oyster tureens, soup and sauce tureen, and a variety of sauce boats. (Be warned not to confuse the teapot for a coffee because of its large size.) Such a profusion of dinnerware implies a considerable household staff. Hudson reflects beautifully an era gone and never to return.

Description points to look for: There is a muted ruffling and embossment around the edges, a touch of curl and scroll on the handles. The hollow ware has a distinctive outward flare at the embossed base allowing for a solid settled look. Jugs, creams, and sugars can be readily recognized by the straight sides which slope outward to the base. I think its most distinctive feature is the knob or finial which has been likened to the shape of a crouching cat. Whatever you may call its shape, it is so distinctive that of all the lid handles shown in this book, it is the one I would never fail to recognize.

Value guide page 98.

Plates 158, 159, and 160: Most pieces of Hudson have the Homer Laughlin stamp on the back and the name Hudson on it. Here are three of the backstamps found on various pieces.

Plate 161: Wood Violets pattern. Part of a large Hudson set lavishly decorated with an abundance of large violets and a dusting of gilt. Shown: individual creamer, 6" plate, coffee cup and saucer, and 9" luncheon plate. The 10" plates are somewhat rare in Hudson; buy them whenever you can.

Plate 162: Hudson 100. Casserole with four butter pats. All are trimmed in grass green and gold. The Hudson in this picture and the set shown above are from the collection of Richard Racheter.

Plates 163 and 164: Hudson 106 (above). calendar plate dated 1909. For some unexplained reason most of the Hudson calendar plates are dated 1909. Gerald DeBolt[2] in his book of marks mentions a 1903 Hudson calendar plate and I have just recently located a 1910 calendar plate. Hudson 107 (below). This plate matches the Angelus Royal Majolica pattern. See page 106 for an explanation of the Royal Majolica pattern on the Angelus shape. [From the collection of Judi Wilfong.]

Plate 165: Hudson 108. Butter dish. [From the collection of Judi Wilfong.]

Plate 166: Hudson 109. 15" dish (platter) with a large, bold flower decal.

HUDSON

Baker, 5"	$8.00	Jug, ¾ pt.	$16.00
Baker, 7"	$12.00	Jug, 1¾ pt.	$20.00
Baker, 8"	$16.00	Jug, ½ pt.	$25.00
Baker, 9"	$18.00	Jug, 2¼ pt.	$30.00
Baker, 10"	$22.00	Jug, 3¼ pt.	$35.00
Baker, 11"	$24.00	Jug, 5 pt.	$40.00
Bone Dish	$8.00	Jug, 6 pt.	$45.00
Bullion Cup, 6oz.	$12.50	Ladle	$22.00
Bullion Saucer	$6.00	Nappy, 6"	$10.00
Bowl, deep, 1 pt.	$11.00	Nappy, 7"	$12.00
Bowl, deep, 1½ pt.	$13.00	Nappy, 8"	$16.00
Butter, covered	$50.00	Nappy, 9"	$20.00
Butter, individual	$5.50	Nappy, 10"	$22.00
Cake Plate	$20.00	Oatmeal, 5¾"	$6.00
Casserole, covered	$45.00	Oatmeal, 6¼"	$7.00
Celery Tray	$25.00	Pickle	$20.00
Coffee Cup	$9.00	Plate (Coupe Soup), 7"	$7.00
Coffee Saucer	$5.00	Plate (Coupe Soup), 8"	$8.00
Coffee Saucer, AD	$6.00	Plate, 6"	$4.50
Coffee, AD	$14.00	Plate, 7"	$5.50
Covered Dish, 8"	$40.00	Plate, 8"	$7.50
Cream	$12.00	Plate, 9"	$8.00
Cream Soup	$16.00	Plate, 10"	$10.00
Cream Soup Stand	$8.00	Plate, deep (Rim Soup), 9"	$9.00
Creamer, individual	$10.00	Salad, Orleans, 7"	$14.00
Dish (Platter), 6"	$8.00	Sauce Boat	$18.00
Dish (Platter), 7"	$10.00	Sauce Boat (Fast Stand)	$22.50
Dish (Platter), 8"	$11.00	Sauce Boat Stand	$9.00
Dish (Platter), 9"	$14.00	Sauce Ladle	$22.00
Dish (Platter), 10"	$16.00	Sauce Tureen Stand	$10.50
Dish (Platter), 11"	$18.00	Sauce Tureen, 6"	$35.00
Dish (Platter), 12"	$20.00	Soup Ladle	$25.00
Dish (Platter), 13"	$22.00	Spooner	$45.00
Dish (Platter), 14"	$23.00	Sugar, covered	$18.00
Dish (Platter), 15"	$24.00	Sugar, individual	$14.00
Dish (Platter), 17"	$26.00	Teacup (only)	$5.00
Egg Cup, Boston	$15.50	Teacup Saucer (only)	$3.00
Fruit, 5"	$5.00	Teapot	$75.00
Fruit, 5¼"	$6.00	Tureen, oyster	$60.00
Jug, 1⅛ pt.	$22.00		

Plate 167: Catalog picture of Hudson.

1 Teapot
2 Sugar
3 Cream
4 Individual Sugar
5 Individual Cream
6 Sauce Boat
7 Bowl
8 Coffee
9 Tea
10 A.D. Coffee
11 Salad

12 Nappy
13 Baker
14 Oatmeal
15 Fruit
16 Individual Butter
17 Bone
18 Pickle
19 Spooner
20 Dish
21 Cake

22 Covered Butter
23 Deep Plate
24 Plate
25 Coupe Soup
26 Oyster Tureen
27 Covered Dish
28 Casserole
29 Sauce Tureen
30 Celery Tray
31 Jug

MAJESTIC

The Majestic shape can be dated to the second decade of the twentieth century. While I have looked at the Majestic backstamp for years, I was never able to associate the mark with the appearance of the shape. A fellow collector sent me a photo of two casseroles (Plate 170) which showed what appeared to be identical casseroles except for the slight difference in the finial shape. I wondered why HLC would make what was clearly Hudson but with different finials. Another collector called to tell me she was sending me a picture of her Majestic casserole. In due time another photo of Hudson arrived. Finally I realized that the Hudson with the funny finial was really the long-sought Majestic. Subsequently, an interesting small platter or sauce boat stand came into my possession, shown in Plate 169. Note the heavily scalloped rim, outlined with the finely embossed pattern. I have since seen a dinner plate, which looks much like Hudson. The relationship of the two shapes is further emphasized by their use of the same embossing. The Majestic shape was probably produced for only a short time, since it has proven rather difficult to find. One has to wonder what market niche HLC was aiming for that was not already covered by the far more common Hudson.

For value guide, use Hudson guide on page 98.

Plate 168: Majestic backstamp. Note that the Majestic shape does not carry a usual HLC mark positively identifying the potter. It could thus be overlooked by a collector who was looking only for wares with a familiar Homer Laughlin marking.

Plate 169: This sauce boat stand or very small platter measures 8".

Plate 170: Majestic 100 (left). Casserole with the Majestic backstamp. Note that the finial is larger than Hudson's and that the "tail" points down. Golden Lace casserole (right) with Hudson backstamp and finial with "tail" pointing out.

ANGELUS

The Angelus shape, a favorite with both Sears, Roebuck & Co. and Montgomery Ward & Co. catalogs, dates from the first decade of the 1900s. I have an invoice for Angelus from the archives of HLC which is dated 1905. It appears in a Sears catalog of 1906. Another invoice from HLC shows that Angelus was still being sold in 1916. Except for the cups, Angelus is usually found marked with its name and is moderately easy to find in antiques stores. The relatively plentiful supplies of Angelus are most likely due to its long production life compared to some other early HLC shapes.

Description of points to look for: Angelus has crinkly handles and finials, which are its most identifying mark. It can also be identified by tiny beading that surrounds its rims. The flatware has a scalloped edge. This shape is found mainly decorated in various types of small flowers of which roses were the favorites of that time.

See value guide on page 104.

Plate 171: Angelus 100. This beautiful photograph of an Angelus teapot was sent to me by Chip Simpson and Jeanie Milburn of Maryland.

Plate 172: Angelus 101. Sauce boat on a sauce boat stand. [From the collection of Judi Wilfong.]

Plate 173: Angelus 102. This Angelus "fish-shaped" pickle was a general favorite. The "tail" makes a very respectable handle. This piece, once thought rare, is turning up more often in antiques stores.

Plate 174: Angelus 103. This butter dish has a very interesting gold design. A good example of Angelus embossing is visible on the rim. [From the collection of Judi Wilfong.]

Plate 175: Angelus 104. A casserole in the familiar small pink roses.

Plate 176: Angelus 105. Shown is the 13" dish (platter). Realistic fruit (here ripe, red cherries) is rather unusual on early Homer Laughlin china. A delicate touch is the inclusion of pink blossoms and scattering of petals at the bottom. [From the collection of Richard Racheter.]

ANGELUS

Baker, 5"	$10.00	Jug, ¾ pt.	$18.00
Baker, 7"	$16.00	Jug, 1⅛ pt.	$22.00
Baker, 8"	$18.00	Jug, 1¾ pt.	$25.00
Baker, 9"	$20.00	Jug, 2¼ pt.	$30.00
Baker, 10"	$22.00	Jug, 3¼ pt.	$35.00
Baker, 11"	$24.00	Jug, 5 pt.	$40.00
Bone Dish	$8.00	Jug, 6 pt.	$45.00
Bullion Cup, 6 oz.	$12.50	Ladle	$22.00
Bullion Saucer	$6.00	Nappy, 6"	$10.00
Bowl, deep, 1 pt.	$11.00	Nappy, 7"	$16.00
Bowl, deep, 1½ pt.	$13.00	Nappy, 8"	$18.00
Butter, covered	$55.00	Nappy, 9"	$20.00
Butter, individual	$6.50	Nappy, 10"	$22.00
Cake Plate	$20.00	Oatmeal, 5¾"	$6.00
Casserole, covered	$45.00	Oatmeal, 6¼"	$7.00
Coffee Cup	$10.00	Pickle (Handle), 8"	$24.00
Coffee Saucer	$6.00	Plate (Coupe Soup), 7"	$7.00
Coffee Saucer, AD	$6.00	Plate (Coupe Soup), 8"	$8.00
Coffee, AD	$16.00	Plate, 6"	$5.00
Covered Dish	$40.00	Plate, 7"	$6.50
Cream	$13.00	Plate, 8"	$7.50
Cream Soup	$15.00	Plate, 9"	$9.00
Cream Soup Stand	$8.00	Plate, 10"	$10.00
Creamer, individual	$10.00	Plate, deep (Rim Soup), 9"	$9.00
Dish (Platter), 6"	$8.00	Salad, Orleans, 7"	$11.00
Dish (Platter), 7"	$10.00	Sauce Boat	$18.00
Dish (Platter), 8"	$11.00	Sauce Boat (Fast Stand)	$24.50
Dish (Platter), 9"	$12.00	Sauce Boat Stand	$10.00
Dish (Platter), 10"	$13.00	Sauce Ladle	$22.00
Dish (Platter), 11"	$14.00	Soup Ladle	$25.00
Dish (Platter), 12"	$16.00	Spoon Holder	$48.00
Dish (Platter), 13"	$20.00	Sugar, covered	$18.00
Dish (Platter), 14"	$22.00	Sugar, individual	$14.00
Dish (Platter), 15"	$24.00	Teacup (only)	$6.00
Dish (Platter), 17"	$28.00	Teacup Saucer (only)	$3.00
Egg Cup, Boston	$15.50	Teapot	$70.00
Fruit, 5"	$5.00	Tureen, oyster, 8"	$65.00
Fruit, 5¼"	$6.00	Tureen, sauce	$35.00
Jug, ½ pt.	$15.00	Tureen, sauce, stand	$10.00

Plate 177: Catalog picture of Angelus.

1 Teapot	8 Tea	15 Individual Butter	22 Coupe Soup
2 Sugar	9 A.D. Coffee	16 Bone Dish	23 Pickle
3 Cream	10 Salad	17 Spooner	24 Oyster Tureen
4 Sauce Boat	11 Nappy	18 Dish	25 Casserole
5 Covered Butter	12 Baker	19 Cake	26 Covered Dish
6 Bowl	13 Oatmeal	20 Plate	27 Sauce Tureen Complete
7 Coffee	14 Fruit	21 Deep Plate	28 Jug

ROYAL MAJOLICA

Royal Majolica is not really a separate shape at all, but rather a special decorative treatment applied to a standard HLC shape of the time. The 1909 Sears Roebuck catalog displayed a full page advertisement for Royal Majolica, the "Scenic Dinner Set." What they don't say is that this is none other than the Homer Laughlin Angelus shape decorated in an interesting and unique manner. Each different piece is decorated with its own special decal depicting some aspect of country life. The smaller platter has people by a bridge. The larger platter has a manor house with a steeple. The large jug shows people on a bridge in front of a farm house, while the smaller jug has a farm house and fields. The different size plates have variations on the farm scenes. The butter top displays an English-style farm house with a young woman in the yard and sailboats in the bottom. (See Plate 179.) Other pieces, when found, will follow this decorative scheme. Unfortunately, the detail shown in the catalog pages does not permit describing the special scene on each piece with any accuracy. However, Royal Majolica can be easily identified by the special backstamp shown in Plate 178. The collector should note that the Royal Majolica decoration was not limited to Angelus. It has also been seen on Colonial (Plate 180) and on Hudson.

For pricing, use the Angelus value guide, page 104, plus 20%.

Plate 179: Royal Majolica Angelus 100. Butter dish in the Angelus shape.

Plate 178: Royal Majolica backstamp.

Plate 180: Royal Majolica Colonial 100. Olive dish in the Colonial shape.

GENESEE

I have not yet found the starting date for Genesee. The HLC files reveal that it was sold to Sperry & Hutchinson, the producers of S&H Green Stamps, in 1911, and that another Homer Laughlin customer who purchased this shape was S.H. Kress in 1912. Genesee probably enjoyed a relatively long production run, since it is almost as easy to find as Hudson.

Description of points to look for: Genesee is a very plain, solid shape which has no embossing at all. Its hollow ware, which is smooth with graceful curves, is identical to the Niagara shape. The flatware has a smooth edge on round and oval shapes (unlike Niagara whose flatware is scalloped). To date, all Genesee I have seen has been marked with its special backstamp, shown in Plate 184.

Value guide page 110.

Plate 181: Genesee 100. 10" plate with an unusual fish decal.

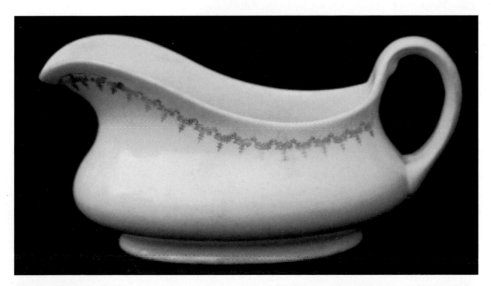

Plate 182: Genesee 101. Sauce boat with gold filigree decoration. A look at the Niagara sauce boat on page 112, Plate 187, will show why one must turn the piece over and examine the backstamp to tell the difference between the two hollow ware shapes.

Plate 183: Genesee 102, above. Notice the pleasing, absolute plainness of the covered dish and of the 16" dish (platter), it is rounded and fuller than platters of other shapes. [From the collection of Richard Racheter.]

Plate 184: Genesee backstamp at right.

Plate 185: Genesee 103, below. Covered casserole and ladle. I found the two together in Cour d'Alene, Idaho, but I wonder if the ladle goes with this shape. I have also seen Hudson with this decoration and its scalloped edges look like it would more likely go with the Hudson shape.

Plate 186: Genesee 104. An 11" Genesee dish (platter), small but charmingly Art Deco.

Plate 187: Genesee 105 (left) and HLC pattern #KR77 (right). Two Genesee jugs standing solid and firm, the smaller, with the gold band, is shown in the HLC files to have been sold by S.H. Kress. The one at the left is decorated with large red roses. [From the collection of Richard Racheter.]

GENESEE

Baker, 4"	$10.00
Baker, 7"	$12.00
Baker, 8"	$14.00
Baker, 9"	$16.00
Baker, 10"	$18.00
Bone Dish	$7.00
Bullion Cup	$14.00
Bullion Saucer	$6.00
Bowl, deep, 1 pt.	$11.00
Bowl, deep, 1½ pt.	$13.00
Butter, covered	$50.00
Butter, individual	$5.50
Cake Plate	$20.00
Casserole, covered, 8"	$40.00
Casserole, covered, 9"	$45.00
Celery Tray	$35.00
Coffee Cup	$12.00
Coffee Saucer	$7.00
Coffee Saucer, AD	$6.00
Coffee, AD	$14.00
Covered Dish, 8"	$35.00
Covered Dish, 9"	$40.00
Cream	$12.00
Cream, individual	$10.00
Dish (Platter), 6"	$8.00
Dish (Platter), 7"	$10.00
Dish (Platter), 8"	$12.00
Dish (Platter), 9"	$14.00
Dish (Platter), 10"	$15.00
Dish (Platter), 12"	$16.00
Dish (Platter), 13"	$18.00
Dish (Platter), 14"	$20.00
Dish (Platter), 15"	$22.00
Dish (Platter), 16"	$25.00
Dish (Platter), 18"	$28.00
Egg Cup, Boston	$17.50
Fruit Bowl	$45.00
Fruit, 5"	$4.00
Fruit, 6"	$7.00
Jug, ¾ pt.	$18.00
Jug, 1 pt.	$22.00
Jug, 1¾ pt.	$25.00
Jug, 2½ pt.	$30.00
Jug, 4 pt.	$35.00
Jug, 5½ pt.	$40.00
Jug, 8 pt.	$55.00
Ladle	$22.00
Nappy, 6"	$8.00
Nappy, 7"	$10.00
Nappy, 8"	$16.00
Nappy, 9"	$18.00
Nappy, 10"	$20.00
Oatmeal, 6"	$6.00
Oatmeal, 6½"	$7.00
Pickle	$20.00
Plate (Coupe Soup), 8"	$8.00
Plate (Coupe Soup), 9"	$9.00
Plate, 6"	$4.50
Plate, 7"	$5.50
Plate, 8"	$7.50
Plate, 9"	$9.00
Plate, 10"	$10.00
Plate, deep (Rim Soup), 9"	$8.00
Sauce Boat	$18.00
Sauce Boat Stand	$9.00
Sauce Boat (Fast Stand)	$25.00
Spoon Holder (Spooner)	$40.00
Sugar, covered	$18.00
Sugar, individual	$10.00
Teacup (only)	$5.00
Teacup Saucer (only)	$3.00
Teapot	$65.00
Tureen Stand	$15.00
Tureen, oyster	$50.00
Tureen, sauce	$35.00
Tureen Stand	$10.00

Plate 188: Catalog picture of Genesee.

1 Teapot	9 A.D. Coffee Cup & Saucer	17 Boston Egg Cup	25 Sauce Boat and Stand
2 Sugar	10 Nappy	18 Spooner	26 Sauce Boat, Fast Stand
3 Cream	11 Coupe Soup	19 Dish	27 Covered Dish
4 Sugar, individual	12 Oatmeal	20 Cake Plate	28 Oyster Tureen
5 Cream, individual	13 Fruit	21 Plate	29 Casserole
6 Covered Butter	14 Individual Butter	22 Baker	30 Sauce Tureen, complete
7 Teacup and Saucer	15 Bone Dish	23 Celery Tray	31 Jug
8 Coffee Cup and Saucer	16 Bowl, deep	24 Pickle	

NIAGARA

The earliest date I found for Niagara was in the Homer Laughlin files, where there is a record of a shipment of Niagara to Sperry & Hutchinson in 1911. I have not found it sold through the major catalog retailers such as Wards and Sears, which may explain why this shape is somewhat rare and difficult to find in antiques stores. Perhaps it was made specifically to be a premium.

Description of points to look for: Just as Empress and Kwaker share the same flatware, Niagara and Genesee share the same hollow ware, so identification of the hollow ware is impossible without a quick "turnover" to look at the mark. The Niagara flatware has groups of three very small scallops distributed about the otherwise smooth rim. The platter in Plate 190 provides a good view of the shape of the flatware. Notice also the indentation just back from the rim. Niagara flatware is not common.

Value guide page 113.

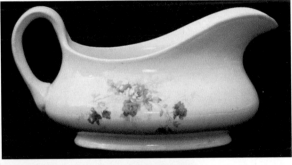

Plate 189: Niagara 100. The sauce boat is identical to the Genesee shape except for the backstamp. [From the collection of Richard Racheter.]

Plate 190: Niagara 101. Measuring 18" by 13", this huge Niagara dish (platter) is never overlooked when displayed. This piece shows the typical ripple effect around the edge. [From the collection of Richard Racheter.]

Plate 191: Niagara 102. The design on this casserole is the same as seen on Empress in the 1925 Butler Bros. catalog, where it is called Virginia. [From the collection of Richard Racheter.]

NIAGARA

Baker, 4"	$8.00
Baker, 7"	$12.00
Baker, 8"	$14.00
Baker, 9"	$16.00
Baker, 10"	$18.00
Bone Dish	$7.00
Bullion Saucer	$8.00
Bowl, deep, 36s	$12.00
Bowl, deep, 30s	$15.00
Butter, covered	$50.00
Butter, individual	$5.00
Cake Plate	$20.00
Casserole, covered, 8"	$35.00
Casserole, covered, 9"	$40.00
Casserole, notched lid	$45.00
Coffee Cup	$10.00
Coffee Saucer	$5.00
Coffee Saucer, AD	$6.00
Coffee, Cup, AD	$12.00
Covered Dish, 8"	$30.00
Covered Dish, 9"	$35.00
Cream	$12.00
Creamer, individual	$10.00
Dish (Platter), 5"	$8.00
Dish (Platter), 6"	$10.00
Dish (Platter), 7"	$11.00
Dish (Platter), 8"	$12.00
Dish (Platter), 9"	$13.00
Dish (Platter), 10"	$14.00
Dish (Platter), 11"	$16.00
Dish (Platter), 12"	$18.00
Dish (Platter), 13"	$20.00
Dish (Platter), 14"	$22.00
Dish (Platter), 16"	$24.00
Dish (Platter), 18"	$26.00
Egg Cup, Boston	$16.00
Fruit, 4½"	$4.00
Fruit, 5"	$5.00
Jug, 48s	$15.00
Jug, 42s	$20.00
Jug, 36s	$30.00
Jug, 30s	$35.00
Jug, 24s	$40.00
Jug, 12s	$45.00
Jug, 6s	$50.00
Nappy, 6"	$10.00
Nappy, 7"	$12.00
Nappy, 8"	$14.00
Nappy, 9"	$16.00
Nappy, 10"	$18.00
Oatmeal, 6"	$6.00
Oatmeal, 6½"	$7.00
Pickle	$15.00
Plate (Coupe Soup), 8"	$7.00
Plate (Coupe Soup), 9"	$8.00
Plate, 6"	$4.50
Plate, 7"	$6.50
Plate, 8"	$7.50
Plate, 9"	$9.00
Plate, 10"	$10.00
Plate, deep (Rim Soup), 9"	$9.00
Sauce Boat	$18.00
Sauce Boat (Fast Stand)	$24.00
Sauce Boat Stand	$8.00
Sauce Ladle	$20.00
Sauce Tureen Stand	$10.00
Spoon Holder (Spooner)	$40.00
Sugar, covered	$16.00
Sugar, individual	$14.00
Teacup (only)	$5.00
Teacup Saucer (only)	$3.00
Teapot	$65.00
Tureen, oyster	$55.00
Tureen, sauce	$30.00

Plate 192: Catalog picture of Niagara.

1 Teapot	8 A.D. Coffee	15 Bowl	22 Pickle
2 Sugar	9 Nappy	16 Boston Egg Cup	23 Sauce Boat and Stand
3 Individual Sugar	10 Baker	17 Spooner	24 Sauce Boat, Fast Stand
4 Cream	11 Oatmeal	18 Dish	25 Casserole
5 Covered Butter	12 Fruit	19 Cake	26 Covered Dish
6 Tea	13 Individual Butter	20 Plate	27 Sauce Tureen, complete
7 Coffee	14 Bone	21 Coupe Soup	28 Jug

Plate 193: Niagara backstamp.

The Knowles, Taylor, Knowles China Company

One of the oldest names on American pottery, Knowles, Taylor, Knowles operated in East Liverpool, Ohio, beginning in the mid-1800s, and remained in operation in East Liverpool until 1931. Isaac Knowles and Isaac Harvey started a factory in East Liverpool, Ohio, in 1854, after operating a store boat on the Ohio and Mississippi Rivers, which sold pottery, glass, and other staples. Their initial factory made yellow ware in a single kiln. Knowles bought out Harvey a couple of years later and operated the factory by himself from 1856 until 1870. In that year John W. Taylor (Isaac's son-in-law) and Homer Knowles (one of Isaac's sons) joined him to form Knowles, Taylor, Knowles. The company became quite large, employing 700 people by 1901. In 1929, KTK was one of eight companies which joined to form the ill-fated American Chinaware Corporation. With the failure of American Chinaware, KTK vanished from the American pottery scene. During their 75 years of operation, KTK brought out not only a wealth of tableware, but the priceless Lotusware as well. A curious footnote to the story of KTK comes from an obituary notice for Homer J. Taylor, in 1943 in Burbank, California:

> "Soon after the dissolution of this merger (i.e., the American Chinaware Corporation) Homer moved with his family to California, where he again engaged in the pottery business, this time manufacturing art ware and ceramic specialties. The old and respected firm name, the Knowles, Taylor, & Knowles Co. was used and this enterprise is continuing under the direction of the family since Homer's death."

For more information about the KTK mark from Southern California, see *Collector's Encyclopedia of Knowles, Taylor & Knowles* by Mary Frank Gaston (Collector Books).

The following pages provide a small sample of the various dinnerware products of this noteworthy pottery.

Plate 194: A copy of a picture of the Knowles, Taylor & Knowles Company taken from a catalog at the East Liverpool Museum of Ceramics.

Plate 195: KTK Commandery 100 on the left and KTK Commandery 101 on the right. Commandery plates made for the Masonic orders to give out for special events. These are just two of a large number made, and are dated 1901. [From the collection of Bill and Donna Gray.]

Suggested value of specialty plates ....$22.00 – 32.00
Suggested valuc of Commandery plates...$45.00 – 65.00

NEVADA

Gates and Ormerod[1] date the backstamp found on the Nevada jug shown in Plate 198 as 1890 – 1907. A postcard on the opposite page in Plate 195 showing the Nevada shape is dated July 15, 1886. Nevada is thus a very early KTK shape made of KTK's version of ironstone, as opposed to the later semiporcelain. The Nevada shape is quite rare today, not surprising in light of its antiquity. I had a Nevada jug which was claimed by the 1994 Northridge earthquake, but I had the good fortune to find another (Plate 198) in Zanesville, Ohio, to replace it.

Description of points to look for: This shape has no embossing and simple scalloped edges. Handles appear very functional and meet in the top corner in a large joint. Finials consist of two pieces which curve up to meet in a similar joint.

For a value guide use St. Louis on page 121. Add 20%.

Plate 196: Nevada backstamp found on the jug in Plate 198.

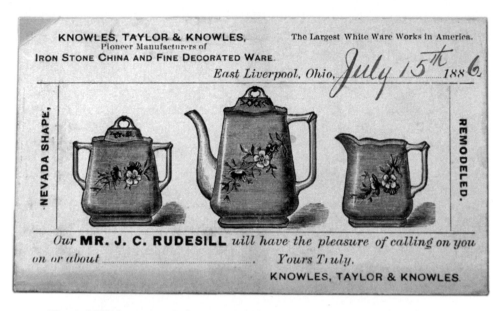

Plate 197: A postcard showing the Nevada sugar, teapot, and creamer.

Plate 198: Nevada 100. Large jug found in Zanesville, Ohio. The decoration is a brown transfer of a favorite of that time, Moss Rose. (See glossary for information about the Moss Rose pattern.) Hand painting completes the roses.

TACOMA

Tacoma, made of ironstone, is one of the earlier KTK shapes. A Tacoma backstamp is dated by Gates and Ormerod[1] ca. 1985 – 1895. There are pages and pages of catalog pictures showing Tacoma patterns in the archives of the East Liverpool Museum of Ceramics. They all show this shape decorated with the subtle colors that came from the transfer designs of that time.

Description of points to look for: Tacoma has a simple finger-imprint style of embossing. The flatware has an edge with a large then a small scallop which repeats itself. The handles and finials are scrolls that meet with another shorter scroll, almost like two hands joining. (See Plate 201.)

For a value guide use St. Louis page 121.

Plate 199: Tacoma 100. Sauce boat stand or pickle in white with gold.

Plate 200: Tacoma from a catalog at the East Liverpool Museum of Ceramics.

Plate 201: Tacoma 101. Sauce boat with brown transfer decoration and hand-painted blue flowers.

ST. LOUIS

This shape is dated in Gates and Ormerod[1] as 1904 – 1906. In the KTK catalog it shares space with a very rare shape called Jefferson. Since no pieces of Jefferson have yet appeared, it was not included in this book. St. Louis is shown in the 1905 Montgomery Ward & Co. catalog in a blue forget-me-not pattern. St. Louis serving pieces turn up regularly in the antiques markets. The same cannot be said for cups, saucers, and plates.

Description of points to look for: St. Louis flatware has an irregular scalloped edge. Its embossing is visible in the catalog pictures on page 122, but the embossing on all the pieces I have seen so far is almost nonexistent. Since the catalog pictures were produced by artists rather than photographed, the pictured embossing can perhaps be attributed to the enthusiasm of the sales department. The platters are easy to spot because they come almost to a point on each end. The finials on casseroles are also easily recognized. They seem to sport a very small pair of horns (see page 122, Plate 205).

Value guide page 121.

Plate 202: Backstamp from the back of a St. Louis platter. All my pieces had the same backstamp.

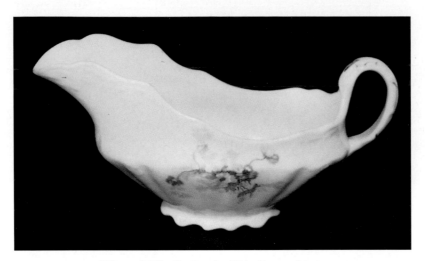

Plate 203: St. Louis 101. Sauce boat.

Plate 204: St. Louis 102. 12½" dish (platter). St. Louis 103. Sauce boat stand.

ST. LOUIS

Baker, 6	$10.00	Dish (Platter), 18"	$26.00
Baker, 7½"	$12.00	Dish (Platter), 19"	$28.00
Baker, 8"	$14.00	Egg Cup, double	$17.50
Baker, 9"	$16.00	Fruit, 5"	$5.00
Baker, 10"	$20.00	Fruit, 6"	$7.00
Baker, 11"	$22.00	Jug, 1 pt.	$20.00
Bone Dish	$8.00	Jug, 2 pt.	$25.00
Bouillon Cup	$12.00	Jug, 3½ pt.	$30.00
Bouillon Saucer	$4.00	Jug, 4½ pt.	$35.00
Bowl, deep, 1 pt.	$12.00	Jug, 6 pt.	$40.00
Bowl, deep, 1½ pt.	$14.00	Jug, 8 pt.	$55.00
Bowl, oyster, 1 pt.	$10.00	Nappy, 6"	$10.00
Bowl, oyster, 1½ pt.	$12.00	Nappy, 7"	$12.00
Butter, covered	$45.00	Nappy, 8"	$16.00
Butter, individual	$5.50	Nappy, 9"	$18.00
Cake Plate	$23.00	Nappy, 10"	$20.00
Casserole, covered, 8"	$40.00	Oatmeal, 6½"	$7.00
Casserole, covered, 9"	$45.00	Pickle	$16.00
Casserole, notched lid	$50.00	Plate (Coupe Soup), 8"	$8.00
Coffee Cup	$12.00	Plate (Coupe Soup), 9"	$9.00
Coffee Saucer	$7.00	Plate, 6"	$4.50
Coffee Saucer, AD	$6.00	Plate, 7"	$5.50
Coffee, AD	$14.00	Plate, 8"	$8.50
Covered Dish, 8"	$35.00	Plate, 9"	$9.00
Covered Dish, 9"	$40.00	Plate, 10"	$10.00
Cream	$12.00	Plate, deep (Rim Soup), 9"	$9.00
Cream, individual	$10.00	Sauce Boat	$20.00
Custard, handled	$16.00	Sauce Boat Stand	$10.00
Custard, unhandled	$14.00	Sauce Boat (Fast Stand)	$24.00
Custard, Ladle	$12.00	Sauce Ladle	$22.00
Dish (Platter), 4½"	$8.00	Sauce Tureen Stand	$10.50
Dish (Platter), 7"	$11.00	Sauce Tureen	$35.00
Dish (Platter), 8½"	$12.00	Spoon Holder (Spooner)	$42.00
Dish (Platter), 9½"	$13.00	Sugar	$18.00
Dish (Platter), 10½"	$14.00	Sugar, individual	$14.00
Dish (Platter), 11½"	$15.00	Teacup (only)	$5.00
Dish (Platter), 12"	$16.00	Teacup Saucer (only)	$3.00
Dish (Platter), 13½"	$17.50	Teapot	$70.00
Dish (Platter), 14½"	$19.00	Tureen Stand	$15.00
Dish (Platter), 16"	$22.00	Tureen, covered	$55.00
Dish (Platter), 17"	$24.00		

BOWLS.

EGG CUPS.

SALADS.

BUTTERS

JUGS

SAUCE BOATS,

BONE DISHES.

SUGARS.

COMPORTS.

NAPPIES

TEA POTS.

OYSTER NAPPIES.

CASSEROLES.

PICKLES.

PLATES

COFFEES.

CREAMS.

Plate 205: Catalog picture of St. Louis.

PLYMOUTH

The Plymouth shape is dated by Gates and Ormerod[1] as ca. 1900 – 1907. That date fits nicely with the picture of this shape in a KTK catalog dated 1905. Plymouth is not as difficult to find as some other early KTK shapes.

Description of points to look for: Close attention should be paid to the flower-like embossing which is best seen on the small plate behind the AD saucer in Plate 206 and in the catalog picture on page 125. Also of note are the four prominent indentations about the edge of the dish (platter). Plymouth hollow ware has flat oval embossed finials.

Value guide page 124.

Plate 206: Plymouth 100. This delicate AD cup and saucer were found in a Southern California store. Again note the unusual flower embossing on the plate.

Plate 207: Plymouth 101. 8" covered dish, one of three sizes the covered dish was made in, was sent to me from Ohio.

Plate 208: Plymouth 102. This 13" dish (platter) which matches the covered dish above was found at a store in Ontario, California.

PLYMOUTH

Baker, 6"	$7.50	Jug, 4½ pt.	$35.00
Baker, 7"	$10.00	Jug, 6 pt.	$40.00
Baker, 8"	$14.00	Jug, 8 pt.	$55.00
Baker, 9"	$16.00	Nappy, 4"	$6.00
Baker, 10"	$20.00	Nappy, 5"	$7.00
Baker, 11"	$24.00	Nappy, 6"	$8.50
Bone Dish	$8.00	Nappy, 7"	$10.00
Bowl, deep, 1¼ pt.	$12.00	Nappy, 8"	$14.00
Bowl, deep, 1½ pt.	$14.00	Nappy, 9"	$16.00
Butter, covered	$55.00	Nappy, 10"	$20.00
Butter, individual	$5.00	Oatmeal, 6"	$7.50
Cake Plate	$25.00	Pickle	$18.00
Casserole, covered	$40.00	Plate (Coupe Soup), 7"	$6.00
Coffee Cup	$8.00	Plate (Coupe Soup), 8"	$7.50
Coffee Saucer	$4.00	Plate, 6"	$5.00
Coffee, Cup, AD	$12.00	Plate, 7"	$6.00
Coffee, Saucer, AD	$6.00	Plate, 8"	$7.50
Covered Dish, 8"	$35.00	Plate, 9"	$9.00
Covered Dish, 9"	$40.00	Plate, 10"	$10.00
Cream	$12.00	Plate, deep (Rim Soup), 8"	$8.00
Dish (Platter), 6"	$10.00	Plate, deep (Rim Soup), 9"	$9.00
Dish (Platter), 7"	$12.50	Plate, deep (Rim Soup), 10"	$10.00
Dish (Platter), 8"	$13.00	Salad, 8"	$20.00
Dish (Platter), 9"	$14.00	Salad, 9"	$25.00
Dish (Platter), 10"	$15.00	Sauce Boat	$20.00
Dish (Platter), 11"	$16.00	Sauce Ladle	$20.00
Dish (Platter), 12"	$17.00	Sauce Tureen	$30.00
Dish (Platter), 13"	$18.50	Sauce Tureen Stand	$10.00
Dish (Platter), 14"	$20.00	Soup Tureen	$55.00
Dish (Platter), 15"	$24.00	Soup Tureen Stand	$12.00
Dish (Platter), 17"	$28.00	Soup Ladle	$25.00
Dish (Platter), 19"	$32.00	Spoon Holder	$40.00
Fruit, 4½"	$4.00	Sugar, covered	$18.00
Fruit, 5"	$5.00	Teacup (only)	$5.00
Fruit, 6"	$6.00	Teacup Saucer (only)	$3.50
Jug, 1 pt.	$18.00	Teapot	$65.00
Jug, 1¼ pt.	$22.00	Tureen, oyster	$60.00
Jug, 2⅛ pt.	$26.00	Oyster Ladle	$22.00
Jug, 3½ pt.	$30.00		

Plate 209: Catalog picture of Plymouth.

PORTLAND

An advertisement in *China, Glass, and Lamps* dated 1905 calls attention to "our new Portland shape dinner set in no. 529 Oriental border decoration." Another advertisement in a 1915 Montgomery Ward & Co. catalog shows three sets of Portland dinnerware for sale: Pink Rose, Oregon Plain White, and Sunrise. The shape seems to have been quite popular, as I have located not only single pieces, but even a very large set, in nearby antiques stores.

Description of points to look for: Portland has a bow-like finial on its lids (see Plate 213). The edge on the flatware is evenly scalloped. I think its most distinctive feature is the tiny beaded edging on the rim. This can be best seen on the plates on the next page.

Value guide on page 128.

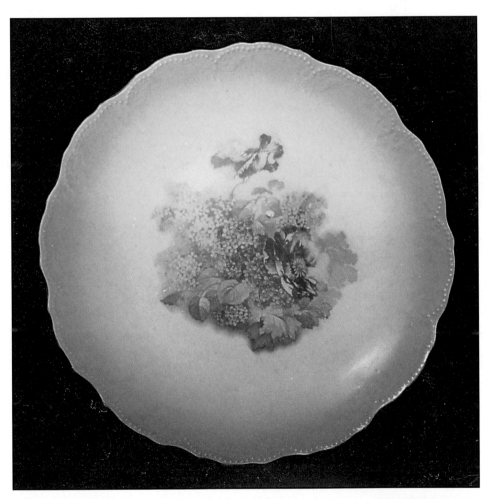

Plate 210: Portland 101. 10" plate that may have been part of a set or, due to its fancy decoration, a specialty plate. This also gives another good look at the bead edging.

Plate 211: Portland 102. 9½" dish (platter) and 8" casserole. The casserole came in two sizes. The casserole was pieced together for this picture after being damaged by the Jan. 17, 1994, Northridge earthquake.

Plate 212: Portland 103. 10" plate, coupe soup, and cup and saucer.

PORTLAND

Baker, 5½"	$8.00	Jug, ¾ pt.	$18.00
Baker, 6"	$10.50	Jug, 1 pt.	$20.00
Baker, 7"	$12.00	Jug, 1½ pt.	$25.00
Baker, 8½"	$16.00	Jug, 3 pt.	$30.00
Baker, 9½	$18.00	Jug, 3¾ pt.	$35.00
Baker, 10½"	$20.00	Jug, 5¾ pt.	$45.00
Baker, 11½	$24.00	Ladle	$22.00
Bone Dish	$8.00	Mint Sauce, 3 oz.	$8.00
Bouillon Cup, 7 oz.	$12.00	Nappy, 6½"	$10.50
Bouillon Saucer	$6.00	Nappy, 7½"	$12.00
Bowl, deep, 1 pt.	$12.00	Nappy, 9"	$16.00
Bowl, deep, 1½ pt.	$14.00	Nappy, 9½"	$18.00
Bowl, deep, 2 pt.	$16.00	Nappy, 10½"	$22.00
Bowl, oyster, ¾ pt.	$10.00	Oatmeal, 5"	$6.50
Bowl, oyster, 1 pt.	$12.00	Oatmeal, 6½"	$7.50
Bowl, oyster, 1¼ pt.	$14.00	Olive, 8"	$15.00
Butter, covered	$65.00	Pickle	$18.00
Butter, individual	$5.00	Plate (Coupe Soup), 7"	$6.00
Cake Plate	$30.00	Plate (Coupe Soup), 8"	$7.50
Casserole, covered	$45.00	Plate (Coupe Soup), 9"	$8.50
Chop Plate, 12"	$25.00	Plate, 6"	$5.00
Coffee Cup	$10.00	Plate, 7"	$6.00
Coffee Saucer	$6.00	Plate, 8"	$7.50
Coffee Cup, AD	$14.00	Plate, 9"	$9.00
Coffee Saucer, AD	$6.00	Plate, 10"	$10.00
Covered Dish, 9"	$35.00	Plate, deep (Rim Soup), 9"	$9.00
Covered Dish, 9½"	$40.00	Ramekin	$10.00
Creamer	$14.00	Ramekin Plate	$6.00
Dish (Platter), 8"	$12.00	Sauce Boat	$20.00
Dish (Platter), 11½"	$16.00	Sauce Boat (Fast Stand)	$26.00
Dish (Platter), 13½"	$17.50	Spoon Tray, 9"	$45.00
Dish (Platter), 15½"	$20.00	Sugar, covered	$18.00
Dish (Platter), 17½"	$28.00	Teacup (only)	$5.00
Dish (Platter), 19½"	$30.00	Teacup Saucer (only)	$3.50
Fruit, 4½"	$4.00	Teapot	$65.00
Fruit, 5"	$5.00	Tureen, oyster	$60.00
Fruit, 6"	$6.00	Tureen, sauce	$35.00

Plate 213: Catalog picture of Portland.

RAMONA

According to Gates and Ormerod[1], Ramona dates from around 1907 to 1915. It is shown in the 1907 Montgomery Ward & Co. catalog and in the October 1908 *American Pottery Gazette* it is called "the daintiest and best dinner ware in America. Plain lines, without embossing and decorated with an original and exclusive design that captivates everyone who sees it." This shape has been found both in large sets and by the piece but only in one case has the name Ramona been found included in the backstamp. On page 119, Plate 202 is the backstamp usually found, while Plate 214 shows a less-common Ramona backstamp. Today, supplies of Ramona are relatively plentiful.

Description of points to look for: As can be easily seen, the Ramona shape is exactly what the *Gazette* says, plain lines without embossing. I think the features which make this shape so special are the elaborate and unusual finials, which can be seen in Plate 217. The handles on some pieces, such as the sugar and creamer, appear to be only partially attached at the bottom (see Plate 217). The casserole handles are split vertically at the top with small balls spaced inside the split.

Value guide on page 133.

Plate 214: Ramona backstamp.

Plate 215: Ramona 102. Three-pint jug with white and gold. Notice the slight protrusion on the upper outside of the handle of this otherwise very plain jug. This point is a good way to identify some Ramona pieces with handles.

Plate 216: Ramona 100. Sauce boat with red and gold decoration. Ramona 101. 13½" dish (platter) with blue vase decal.

Plate 217: Ramona shape pattern #309. Covered dish, creamer, and sugar with a lovely green decoration.

Plate 218: Ramona shape pattern #309. Butter dish and butter pats. The butter pats had the Ramona back-stamp. Unfortunately, putting a back-stamp of any kind on the butter pats was not a usual practice by potters. I wonder how many butter pats for old china sets I've passed up because they didn't have backstamps.

Plate 219: This Ramona covered dish picture was found on the second page of the KTK catalog. It helps identify the covered dish pictured below. It looks like Ramona but the finial is different from the usual Ramona finial (see Plate 218 for good look at the usual finial). It remains unclear why KTK made two different finials, but perhaps they felt there may have been a market for a less formal dinnerware.

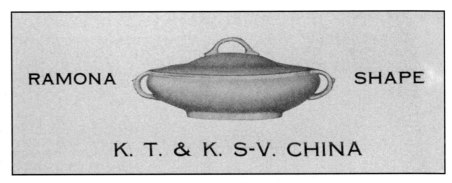

Plate 220: Ramona 103. Covered dish with a much plainer finial. If you look close-ly you can see the split handles that mark the Ramona dishes. The split starts right above the small round balls on the handle and widens up to where it attaches to the rim.

RAMONA

Baker, 5½"	$8.00	Jug, ¾ pt.	$15.00
Baker, 6"	$10.50	Jug, 1 pt.	$18.00
Baker, 7"	$14.00	Jug, 1½ pt.	$22.00
Baker, 8½"	$16.00	Jug, 3 pt.	$26.00
Baker, 9½	$18.00	Jug, 3¾ pt.	$30.00
Baker, 10½"	$24.00	Jug, 5¾ pt.	$40.00
Baker, 11½	$26.00	Ladle	$22.00
Bone Dish	$8.00	Mint Sauce, 3 oz.	$8.00
Bouillon Cup, 7 oz.	$12.00	Nappy, 6½"	$10.50
Bouillon Saucer	$6.00	Nappy, 7½"	$14.00
Bowl, deep, 1 pt.	$12.00	Nappy, 9"	$16.00
Bowl, deep, 1½ pt.	$14.00	Nappy, 9½"	$18.00
Bowl, deep, 2 pt.	$16.00	Nappy, 10½"	$24.00
Bowl, oyster, ¾ pt.	$10.00	Oatmeal, 5"	$6.50
Bowl, oyster, 1 pt.	$12.00	Oatmeal, 6½"	$7.50
Bowl, oyster, 1¼ pt.	$14.00	Olive, 8"	$15.00
Butter, covered	$65.00	Pickle	$18.00
Butter, individual	$6.00	Plate (Coupe Soup), 7"	$6.00
Cake Plate	$30.00	Plate (Coupe Soup), 8"	$7.50
Casserole, covered	$45.00	Plate (Coupe Soup), 9"	$8.50
Chop Plate, 12"	$30.00	Plate, 6"	$5.00
Coffee Cup	$10.00	Plate, 7"	$6.00
Coffee Saucer	$6.00	Plate, 8"	$7.50
Coffee, Cup, AD	$14.00	Plate, 9"	$9.00
Coffee, Saucer, AD	$6.00	Plate, 10"	$10.00
Covered Dish, 9"	$35.00	Plate, deep (Rim Soup), 9"	$9.00
Covered Dish, 9½"	$40.00	Ramekin	$10.00
Cream	$14.00	Ramekin Plate	$6.00
Dish (Platter), 8"	$12.00	Sauce Boat	$20.00
Dish (Platter), 11½"	$16.00	Sauce Boat (Fast Stand)	$26.00
Dish (Platter), 13½"	$17.50	Spoon Tray, 9"	$45.00
Dish (Platter), 15½"	$20.00	Sugar, covered	$18.00
Dish (Platter), 17½"	$24.00	Teacup (only)	$5.00
Dish (Platter), 19½"	$28.00	Teacup Saucer (only)	$3.50
Fruit, 4½"	$4.50	Teapot	$75.00
Fruit, 5"	$5.00	Tureen, oyster	$65.00
Fruit, 6"	$6.00	Tureen, sauce	$35.00

Plates 221 and 222: Catalog pictures of Ramona.

AMERICA

The America shape was brought out around 1909. The decals on the pieces shown below reflect the decorative tastes of the times. These elaborate bands were used on much of the china from the early teens to 1920s.

Description of points to look for: America has no embossing. It has a simple, handle-like finial. Notice that the lids on the hollow ware are recessed into the body, rather than sitting atop or sometimes overhanging (see Plate 223). Also notice that the pickle (page 137, row three) has rectangular handles whereas the olive, celery tray (page 137, row one), and cake plate have pointed handles. The flatware has smooth edges in both round and oval shapes. The America flatware can easily be confused with the KTK Victory shape on page 140 and Niana shape page 146.

Value guide page 136.

Plate 223: America 100. 13" dish (platter), covered dish, and 9" nappy with a band of pink roses on black background set between sections of blue.

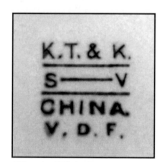

Plate 224: Backstamp found on America shape platter shown at left. DeBolt[2] dates this mark as 1920.

Plate 225: America 101. 11" dish (platter) and pickle. The pickle, decorated with bands of red, blue, and pink flowers, can also be used also as an under dish for the sauce boat. America 103. A sauce boat with a slightly different style of band decoration than the platter and pickle.

AMERICA

Baker, 5½"	$8.50	Fruit, 4½"	$3.50
Baker, 7"	$12.00	Fruit, 5"	$4.00
Baker, 8"	$14.00	Fruit, 5½"	$4.50
Baker, 9"	$16.50	Fruit, 6"	$5.00
Baker, 10"	$18.00	Grapefruit	$4.50
Baker, 11"	$22.00	Hot Water, covered, 8 oz.	$45.00
Bouillon Cup, 7 oz.	$10.00	Jug, 15 oz.	$22.00
Bouillon Saucer	$6.00	Jug, 1½ pt.	$28.00
Bowl, deep, 19 oz.	$14.00	Jug, 2¼ pt.	$30.00
Bowl, deep, 1½ pt.	$16.00	Jug, 3 pt.	$35.00
Bowl, oyster, ¾ pt.	$10.00	Jug, 4 pt.	$40.00
Bowl, oyster, 1 pt.	$12.00	Jug, 5 pt.	$45.00
Bowl, oyster, 1¼ pt.	$14.00	Mayonnaise Bowl (Fast Stand)	$35.00
Butter, covered	$45.00	Muffin Cover	$45.00
Butter, individual	$5.00	Muffin Plate	$15.00
Butter, open tub	$75.00	Nappy, 7"	$12.00
Cake Plate	$20.00	Nappy, 8"	$14.00
Casserole, covered, 7"	$30.00	Nappy, 9"	$16.00
Casserole, covered, 9"	$35.00	Nappy, 9½"	$18.00
Celery Tray, 13"	$15.00	Nappy, 11½"	$24.00
Cheese & Cracker Dish	$75.00	Oatmeal, 6"	$6.00
Chocolate Cup, 4½ oz.	$9.00	Oatmeal, 6½"	$7.50
Chocolate Saucer	$4.50	Olive, 8"	$14.50
Coffee Cup	$8.00	Oyster Ladle	$22.00
Coffee Pot, individual	$35.00	Pickle	$16.50
Coffee Pot, side handle	$95.00	Plate (Coupe Soup), 8"	$7.00
Coffee Saucer	$4.00	Plate (Coupe Soup), 9"	$8.00
Coffee Saucer, AD	$6.00	Plate, 6"	$5.00
Coffee, Cup, AD	$14.00	Plate, 7"	$6.00
Covered Dish, 9"	$35.00	Plate, 8"	$7.50
Cream	$13.50	Plate, 9"	$8.00
Cream Soup	$14.00	Plate, 10"	$10.00
Cream Soup Stand	$6.00	Plate, deep (Rim Soup), 8"	$7.50
Cream, individual	$12.00	Plate, deep (Rim Soup), 9"	$8.00
Custard, handled	$16.00	Ramekin	$8.00
Custard, unhandled	$12.00	Ramekin Plate	$4.50
Dish (Platter), 7"	$8.00	Salad Bowl	$30.00
Dish (Platter), 8"	$10.00	Sauce Boat	$18.50
Dish (Platter), 9"	$12.00	Sauce Boat (Fast Stand)	$24.00
Dish (Platter), 10"	$14.00	Sauce Ladle	$18.00
Dish (Platter), 11"	$16.00	Sauce Tureen, Fast Stand	$35.00
Dish (Platter), 12"	$17.00	Spoon Holder (Spooner)	$45.00
Dish (Platter), 13"	$18.00	Spoon Rest	$35.00
Dish (Platter), 14"	$20.00	Sugar, covered	$16.00
Dish (Platter), 15"	$22.00	Sugar, individual	$13.00
Dish (Platter), 16"	$24.00	Teacup (only)	$4.00
Dish (Platter), 17"	$26.00	Teacup Saucer (only)	$3.00
Dish (Platter), 18"	$28.00	Teapot	$45.00
Dish (Platter), 20"	$35.00	Tureen Stand	$12.00
Egg Cup	$12.00	Tureen, oyster	$40.00
Egg Cup, footed	$16.00	Tureen, sauce	$25.00

BAKERS.

CHOCOLATE POTS.

JUGS.

BOUILLONS.

CHOCOLATES.

NAPPIES.

BOWLS.

BUTTERS.

COFFEE POTS.

PICKLES.

CASSEROLES.

CREAMS.

SAUCE BOATS.

CELERY TRAYS.

America Dish.

SUGARS.

COVERED DISHES.

TEAS.

CHEESE AND CRACKER DISH.

DEEP PLATES.

TEA POTS.

Plate 226: Catalog picture of America.

VICTORY

This shape, which can be dated as early as 1909, is featured in the Montgomery Wards catalog in 1928 in the Blue Bird decal, a favorite of collectors today. It was also shown in the Butler Bros. catalog in 1925 in many different patterns including Golden Rose which had large gold stamped rose sprays; Royal Rose, rose sprays combined with royal blue and tan scrolls and a royal blue hairline band; Royal, a gold leaf design border between royal blue bands; and Flower Basket, a blue basket with natural colored flowers, wide blue band edges, and an inner blue verge line and blue on handles and finial. With so many patterns shown in the various catalogs, it is easy to see why this shape is found so frequently in antiques stores and flea markets.

Descriptive points to look for: Victory has no embossing. There are knob-like finials resembling small Chinese hats. The flatware pieces are round or oval with smooth edges.

Value guide page 139.

Plate 227: Victory 100. 13" platter, casserole, sugar and fast stand sauce boat in the band decal which was a favored decoration of the time.

Plate 228: Victory 101. Three-pint jug resembles two pieces rather than one. It looks like a large sauce boat set on a pedestal.

Plate 229: Victory 102. Creamer with a wide band of pink flowers and black under tan swirls. Victory 103. Covered dish with exotic bird decal.

VICTORY

Baker, 5½"	$8.50	Fruit, 5½"	$5.50
Baker, 8"	$14.00	Grapefruit	$10.50
Baker, 9"	$16.50	Jug, 9 oz.	$16.00
Baker, 10"	$18.00	Jug, 15 oz.	$18.00
Baker, 11"	$22.00	Jug, ⅝ pt.	$20.00
Bouillon Cup, 7 oz.	$10.00	Jug, 1½ pt.	$25.00
Bouillon Saucer	$6.00	Jug, 3 pt.	$30.00
Bowl, deep, 19 oz.	$10.00	Jug, 4 pt.	$35.00
Bowl, deep, 1⅛ pt.	$12.00	Ladle	$22.00
Bowl, deep, 1⅝ pt.	$14.50	Muffin Cover	$55.00
Bowl, oyster, 1 pt.	$10.00	Muffin Plate	$15.00
Bowl, oyster, 1¼ pt.	$12.00	Nappy, 7"	$12.00
Butter, covered	$55.00	Nappy, 8"	$14.00
Butter, individual	$4.00	Nappy, 9"	$16.00
Butter, open tub	$75.00	Nappy, 10"	$18.00
Cake Plate	$25.00	Nappy, 11"	$22.00
Casserole, covered, 9"	$40.00	Oatmeal, 6"	$6.00
Celery Tray, 13"	$15.00	Olive, 8"	$14.50
Coffee Cup	$10.00	Pickle	$18.50
Coffee Saucer	$6.00	Plate (Coupe Soup), 6"	$6.00
Coffee Saucer, AD	$6.00	Plate (Coupe Soup), 7"	$7.00
Coffee, Cup, AD	$14.00	Plate, 6"	$5.00
Covered Dish, 9"	$40.00	Plate, 7"	$6.00
Cream	$13.50	Plate, 8"	$7.50
Cream, individual	$12.00	Plate, 9"	$8.00
Custard, handled	$14.50	Plate, 9½"	$9.00
Custard, unhandled	$12.00	Plate, deep (Rim Soup), 8"	$7.50
Dish (Platter), 8"	$10.00	Plate, deep (Rim Soup), 9"	$8.00
Dish (Platter), 9"	$12.00	Sauce Boat	$18.50
Dish (Platter), 10"	$14.00	Sauce Boat (Fast Stand)	$24.00
Dish (Platter), 11"	$16.00	Sugar, covered	$18.00
Dish (Platter), 13"	$15.00	Sugar, individual	$13.00
Dish (Platter), 14½"	$24.00	Teacup (only)	$5.00
Dish (Platter), 16"	$20.00	Teacup Saucer (only)	$3.00
Egg Cup	$12.00	Teapot	$65.00
Egg Cup, double	$14.00	Tureen Stand	$12.00
Egg Cup, footed	$18.00	Tureen, oyster	$60.00
Fruit, 4½"	$4.50	Tureen, sauce	$30.00
Fruit, 5"	$5.00		

BAKERS—FOOTED.

DISHES—FOOTED.

PLATES.

BOWLS

JUGS.

BUTTERS

SUGARS.

PICKLES.

TEA POTS.

CELERY TRAYS.

NAPPIES.

TEAS.

CREAMS.

SAUCE BOATS.

Plate 230: Catalog picture of Victory.

LOTUS

The KTK Lotus shape is not to be confused with KTK Lotus Ware, a belleek porcelain which today can be found in the hands of museums and wealthy collectors. Lotus Ware was made briefly during the 1890s as a decorative item rather than as utilitarian dinnerware. A KTK catalog for the Lotus shape is in the files of the East Liverpool Museum of Ceramics. Unfortunately, this catalog shows only a few examples of this unusual shape. What the catalog lacks, however, can be found in real life in the antiques malls today, for Lotus is easy to locate, at least by the piece. It has been found in Florida, Ohio, and here on the West Coast. Lotus is shown in the 1915 Montgomery Ward & Co. catalog, where we read that one set of this shape comes in a white and gold pattern which features an initial in the center. Another set could be purchased in Arbutus, a floral pattern. (See Plate 232.) Six years later, in 1921, they were still advertising Lotus in the Arbutus pattern.

Description of points to look for: The easiest way to identify the Lotus shape is by its embossed ridge around the rim (see Plate 235 on page 142 for details of this embossing). The finial on the lid of the casserole and covered dish is another good way to instantly spot Lotus. It was formed as part of the lid rather than something put on after. The sugar and butter have the same finial with the handles on the sugar identical to the handle on the creamer in Plate 233. The sauce boat handle is similar but somewhat shorter and wider. The flatware has a series of large scallops interspersed with small scallops.

Value guide page 143.

Plate 231: Lotus 100. 12" dish (platter) and 9" covered dish in white and gold.

Plate 232: Arbutus 100. 10" plate with green arbutus flower decoration.

Plate 233: Lotus 101. Celery tray. It is very hard to see but there is a thin green line that runs around the rim between the edge and the gold decoration. Lotus 102. Creamer with small blue flowers.

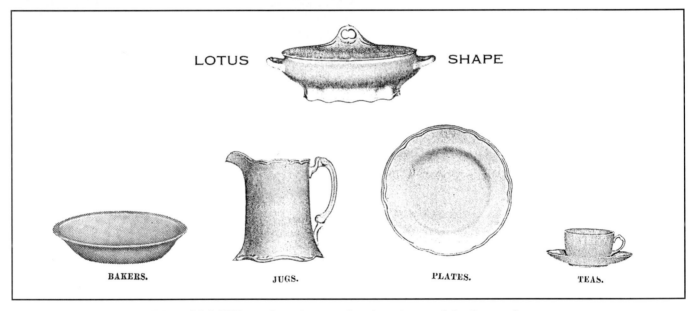

LOTUS   SHAPE

BAKERS.   JUGS.   PLATES.   TEAS.

Plate 234: KTK catalog pictures showing pieces of the Lotus shape.

Plate 235: Close-up of the ridge-like embossing on the Lotus shape.

LOTUS

Baker, 5"	$8.00	Fruit, 5"	$5.00
Baker, 5½"	$10.50	Fruit, 5½"	$5.50
Baker, 7"	$14.00	Fruit, 6½"	$6.50
Baker, 8"	$16.00	Jug, 9 oz.	$14.00
Baker, 9"	$18.50	Jug, 13 oz.	$18.00
Baker, 10"	$20.00	Jug, 21 oz.	$22.00
Baker, 11"	$22.00	Jug, 3½ pt.	$30.00
Bouillon Cup, 8 oz.	$10.00	Jug, 4 pt.	$35.00
Bouillon Saucer	$6.00	Jug, 6¼ pt.	$40.00
Bowl, deep, 1⅛ pt.	$10.00	Ladle	$20.00
Bowl, deep, 1⅝ pt.	$14.50	Nappy, 6½"	$12.00
Bowl, deep, 2 pt.	$16.00	Nappy, 7½"	$14.00
Bowl, oyster, 36s	$10.00	Nappy, 8½"	$16.00
Bowl, oyster, 30s	$13.00	Nappy, 9½"	$18.00
Butter, covered	$55.00	Nappy, 10½"	$20.00
Butter, individual	$4.00	Oatmeal, 6"	$6.00
Casserole, covered, 9"	$35.00	Oatmeal, 6½"	$7.00
Casserole, notched lid	$45.00	Olive, 8"	$14.50
Celery Tray, 13"	$15.00	Pickle	$18.50
Chop Plate, 12"	$30.00	Plate (Coupe Soup), 7"	$6.00
Coffee Cup	$6.00	Plate (Coupe Soup), 8"	$7.00
Coffee Saucer	$4.00	Plate, 6"	$5.00
Coffee Saucer, AD	$6.00	Plate, 7"	$6.00
Coffee, AD	$14.00	Plate, 8"	$7.50
Covered Dish, 9"	$35.00	Plate, 9"	$8.00
Covered Dish, 10"	$40.00	Plate, 10"	$9.00
Creamer	$13.50	Plate, deep (Rim Soup), 9"	$8.00
Dish (Platter), 8"	$10.00	Sauce Boat	$16.50
Dish (Platter), 9"	$12.00	Sauce Boat (Fast Stand)	$20.00
Dish (Platter), 10"	$14.00	Spoon Tray, 9"	$25.50
Dish (Platter), 11"	$16.00	Sugar, covered	$16.00
Dish (Platter), 12"	$16.50	Teacup (only)	$4.00
Dish (Platter), 13½"	$15.00	Teacup Saucer (only)	$3.00
Dish (Platter), 16"	$20.00	Teapot	$45.00
Dish (Platter), 17½"	$24.00	Tureen Stand	$12.00
Dish (Platter), 20"	$30.00	Tureen, oyster	$50.00

NIANA

This simple shape is shown in the Montgomery Wards catalogs in 1915 and 1921. Gates and Ormerod[1] date a Niana backstamp containing the name of the shape from around 1909 to 1915, but I have yet to see a piece with a backstamp of this type. In early years bands of decoration on this shape were favored, while in later years decorations such as blue birds, bunches of roses, and pendants of blue and green were more widely used. Several pattern names found in the Wards catalog are Argyle, a band of sepia with floral scrolls, and Colfax, a band of green leaves and medallions.

Descriptive points to look for: Niana has no embossing. The hollow ware pieces are recognized by their upright sides, which give them a rectangular silhouette. The finial is a simple arch on most of the lids (the coffee pot and covered jug look like they have a round type of knob). Flatware is a smooth-edged round or oval.

Value guide page 145.

Plate 236: Niana 100. Cup and saucer with band of medallions.

Plate 237: Backstamp from Niana saucer.

Plate 238: Niana 101. Covered dish with flowers in a band.

NIANA

Baker, 5½"	$8.50	Fruit, 4½"	$2.50
Baker, 7"	$12.00	Fruit, 5"	$3.00
Baker, 8"	$14.00	Fruit, 5½"	$3.50
Baker, 9"	$16.50	Fruit, 6"	$4.00
Baker, 10"	$18.00	Grapefruit	$4.50
Baker, 11"	$24.00	Hot Water, covered, 8 oz.	$45.00
Bouillon Cup, 7 oz.	$10.00	Jug, 15 oz.	$22.00
Bouillon Saucer	$6.00	Jug, 1½ pt.	$28.00
Bowl, deep, 19 oz.	$12.00	Jug, 2¼ pt.	$30.00
Bowl, deep, 1½ pt.	$14.00	Jug, 3 pt.	$35.00
Bowl, oyster, ¾ pt.	$10.00	Jug, 4 pt.	$40.00
Bowl, oyster, 1 pt.	$14.00	Jug, 5 pt.	$45.00
Bowl, oyster, 1¼ pt.	$16.00	Mayonnaise Bowl (Fast Stand)	$30.00
Butter, covered	$55.00	Muffin Cover	$35.00
Butter, individual	$4.00	Muffin Plate	$20.00
Butter, open tub	$75.00	Nappy, 7"	$10.00
Cake Plate	$25.00	Nappy, 8"	$14.00
Casserole, covered, 7"	$30.00	Nappy, 9"	$16.00
Casserole, covered, 9"	$35.00	Nappy, 9½"	$18.00
Celery Tray, 13"	$15.00	Nappy, 11½"	$26.00
Cheese & Cracker Dish	$75.00	Oatmeal, 6"	$5.00
Chocolate Cup, 4½ oz.	$9.00	Oatmeal, 6½"	$6.50
Chocolate Saucer	$3.50	Olive, 8"	$14.50
Coffee Cup	$6.00	Oyster Ladle	$22.00
Coffee Pot, individual	$25.00	Pickle	$12.50
Coffee Pot, side handle	$95.00	Plate (Coupe Soup), 8"	$7.00
Coffee Saucer	$4.00	Plate (Coupe Soup), 9"	$8.00
Coffee Saucer, AD	$6.00	Plate, 6"	$5.00
Coffee, AD	$14.00	Plate, 7"	$6.00
Covered Dish, 9"	$35.00	Plate, 8"	$7.50
Cream	$13.50	Plate, 9"	$8.00
Cream Soup	$15.00	Plate, 10"	$10.00
Cream Soup Stand	$8.00	Plate, deep (Rim Soup), 8"	$7.50
Cream, individual	$12.00	Plate, deep (Rim Soup), 9"	$8.00
Custard, handled	$8.00	Ramekin	$9.00
Custard, unhandled	$6.00	Ramekin Plate	$4.50
Dish (Platter), 7"	$8.00	Salad Bowl	$30.00
Dish (Platter), 8"	$10.00	Sauce Boat	$18.50
Dish (Platter), 9"	$12.00	Sauce Boat (Fast Stand)	$24.00
Dish (Platter), 10"	$14.00	Sauce Ladle	$16.00
Dish (Platter), 11"	$16.00	Sauce Tureen, Fast Stand	$35.00
Dish (Platter), 12"	$17.00	Spoon Holder (Spooner)	$45.00
Dish (Platter), 13"	$18.00	Spoon Rest	$25.00
Dish (Platter), 14"	$20.00	Sugar, covered	$18.00
Dish (Platter), 15"	$22.00	Sugar, individual	$13.00
Dish (Platter), 16"	$24.00	Teacup (only)	$4.00
Dish (Platter), 17"	$26.00	Teacup Saucer (only)	$3.00
Dish (Platter), 18"	$28.00	Teapot	$45.00
Dish (Platter), 20"	$35.00	Tureen Stand	$12.00
Egg Cup	$12.00	Tureen, oyster	$40.00
Egg Cup, Footed	$18.00	Tureen, sauce	$25.00

BAKERS.

COVERED DISHES.

JUGS.

BOUILLONS.

COFFEE POTS.

NAPPIES.

BOWLS.

Hot Water Jug.

BUTTERS.

PLATES.

CASSEROLES.

COFFEES.

PICKLES.

CELERY TRAYS.

CREAMS.

SAUCE BOATS.

CHEESE AND CRACKER DISH.

DISHES.

SUGARS.

Plate 239: Catalog picture of Niana.

TRAYMORE

Gates and Ormerod[1] date a Traymore backstamp at 1916. Traymore is shown in the 1925 Butler Bros. catalog with the pattern name Staple which was a plain white pattern. This shape was made until 1931 as seen in the backstamp shown below in Plate 240. In 1929 KTK joined with seven other companies in a short-lived attempt to avoid dissolution. This combination was called The American Chinaware Corporation and it lasted less than three years. This backstamp must therefore have been on some of the last pieces made.

Description of points to look for: The Traymore shape was KTK's Haviland look-alike, the familiar embossing on the edge is best seen on the pieces of china in Plate 241. The finial and handles, which look easy to hold, are simple loops. The flatware has an irregular scalloped edge.

Value guide page 148.

Plate 240. Traymore, carrying marks of both KTK and American Chinaware Corp. Note that the KTK mark is dated 1930, while the American Chinaware mark is 1931.

Plate 241. Traymore 100. 10" plate, 8" plate, and fruit.

Plate 242. Dinner set shown in the 1927 Larkin catalog.[5]

TRAYMORE

Baker, 6"	$8.00	Jug, ½ pt.	$18.00
Baker, 7½"	$12.00	Jug, 1¼ pt.	$25.00
Baker, 8½"	$14.00	Jug, 2¼ pt.	$30.00
Baker, 9½"	$16.50	Jug, 3 pt.	$35.00
Baker, 10½"	$20.00	Jug, 4 pt.	$40.00
Baker, 11"	$22.00	Jug, 6¼ pt.	$45.00
Bone Dish	$7.00	Nappy, 7"	$14.00
Bouillon Cup, 7 oz.	$10.00	Nappy, 8"	$16.00
Bouillon Saucer	$6.00	Nappy, 9"	$18.00
Bowl, deep, 1 pt.	$10.00	Nappy, 10"	$20.00
Bowl, deep, 1⅜ pt.	$12.00	Nappy, 11"	$23.00
Bowl, deep, 1⅝ pt.	$11.50	Oatmeal, 6"	$6.00
Butter, covered	$50.00	Pickle	$15.50
Butter, individual	$4.00	Plate (Coupe Soup), 7"	$6.00
Casserole, covered, 9"	$35.00	Plate (Coupe Soup), 8"	$7.00
Coffee Cup	$8.00	Plate, 6"	$5.00
Coffee Saucer	$4.00	Plate, 7"	$6.00
Coffee Saucer, AD	$6.00	Plate, 8"	$7.50
Coffee, Cup, AD	$12.00	Plate, 9"	$8.00
Covered Dish, 10"	$40.00	Plate, 10"	$9.00
Cream	$12.50	Plate, deep (Rim Soup), 9"	$8.00
Dish (Platter), 8"	$10.00	Sauce Boat	$18.50
Dish (Platter), 10"	$14.00	Sauce Boat (Fast Stand)	$24.00
Dish (Platter), 11"	$16.00	Spoon Tray, 9"	$35.50
Dish (Platter), 12"	$16.50	Sugar, covered	$16.00
Dish (Platter), 14"	$15.00	Sugar, individual	$13.00
Dish (Platter), 16"	$20.00	Teacup (only)	$4.00
Dish (Platter), 17½"	$24.00	Teacup Saucer (only)	$3.00
Fruit, 5"	$5.00	Teapot	$45.00
Jug, 13 oz.	$16.00		

Plate 243: Catalog picture of Traymore.

The Edwin M. Knowles China Company

Edwin Knowles, the youngest son of Isaac Knowles (one of the founders of Knowles, Taylor, Knowles China Company), decided to strike out on his own, and in 1900 founded the Edwin M. Knowles China Company. This company erected a new plant in Chester, West Virginia, just across the river from the famous china-making town of East Liverpool, Ohio. While the actual manufacturing operations were conducted in Chester, the company maintained offices in East Liverpool.

In 1913 another plant was built in Newell, West Virginia, another town of the East Liverpool china-making region. This plant was considered at the time to be the most modern and best designed in the district. In 1931, the Chester buildings were sold to the Harker Pottery Company, and all manufacturing operations were then conducted at the Newell plant.

According to an article written in 1937, the Edwin M. Knowles company was the second-largest dinnerware manufacturing company in the United States. (Homer Laughlin was the largest.) They were noted for quality semiporcelain dinnerware, jugs, toilet ware, and hotel ware. By 1940, the company was the third largest china-making company in the United States, employing roughly 900 people. However, the company fell victim to the massive imports from Japan, and in September of 1963 closed its doors forever. The corporation was dissolved, its assets were liquidated, and the Edwin M. Knowles China Company became history. For better or worse, the Edwin Knowles name lives on. The rights to the name were purchased by a distributor of collector plates who has no association whatsoever with the East Liverpool district.

Edwin M. Knowles china was sold through some of the larger mail-order sources such as Montgomery Wards and Butler Brothers.

Plates 244, 245, 246, and 247: Some interesting advertisements featuring the Mayflower shape produced by the Edwin M. Knowles China Company. [From the archives of the East Liverpool Museum of Ceramics.]

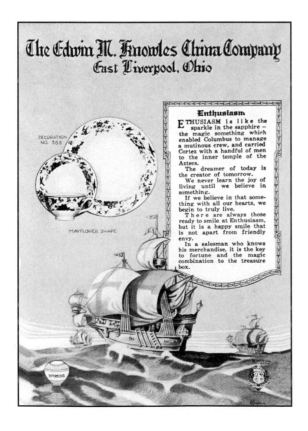

Plate 248: The Edwin Knowles factory in Chester, West Virginia.

Plate 249: The Edwin Knowles factory in Newell, West Virginia.

ARLINGTON

Dating from 1901, this was the earliest Edwin Knowles shape to be made. It is shown in the *China, Glass, and Lamps* trade magazine in 1902, and in the Montgomery Wards catalog in 1906 with a pattern called Florence Rose.

Descriptive points to look for: Arlington has leaf-like embossing (see Plate 252 for a good look at the embossing). Its most distinctive feature is the very unusual finial that looks like a small Chinese pagoda. The Arlington flatware has an irregular scalloped edge.

Value guide page 153.

Plate 250: Arlington 100. This sugar with its lid is decorated with pink flowers.

Plate 251: Arlington 101. Casserole with brown transfer decoration and hand-painted pink and yellow flowers. This and the sugar above were found in the West Virginia area.

ARLINGTON

Baker, 6"	$8.00	Fruit, 5"	$5.50
Baker, 6½"	$10.50	Fruit, 6"	$6.00
Baker, 7½"	$14.00	Jug, 1 pt.	$20.00
Baker, 8"	$16.00	Jug, 2 pt.	$25.00
Baker, 9"	$18.00	Jug, 3 pt.	$30.00
Baker, 10"	$22.00	Jug, 4 pt.	$40.00
Baker, 11"	$24.00	Jug, 6 pt.	$50.00
Bone Dish	$8.00	Jug, 8 pt.	$60.00
Bowl, deep, 1 pt.	$12.00	Nappy, 5"	$8.00
Bowl, deep, 1½ pt.	$14.00	Nappy, 6"	$10.50
Bowl, deep, 2 pt.	$16.00	Nappy, 7"	$14.00
Bowl, oyster, 1 pt.	$10.00	Nappy, 8"	$16.00
Bowl, oyster, 1½ pt.	$12.00	Nappy, 9"	$18.00
Bowl, oyster, 2 pt.	$14.00	Nappy, 10"	$22.00
Butter, covered	$65.00	Nappy, 10½"	$24.00
Butter, individual	$5.00	Oatmeal, 5"	$6.50
Cake Plate	$0.00	Oatmeal, 6½"	$7.50
Casserole, covered, 8"	$40.00	Pickle	$18.00
Casserole, covered, 9"	$45.00	Plate (Coupe Soup), 7"	$6.00
Casserole, notched cover	$50.00	Plate (Coupe Soup), 8"	$7.50
Coffee Cup	$10.00	Plate, 6"	$5.00
Coffee Saucer	$6.00	Plate, 7"	$6.00
Coffee, Cup, AD	$12.00	Plate, 8"	$7.50
Coffee Saucer, AD	$6.00	Plate, 9"	$9.00
Comport	$65.00	Plate, 10"	$10.00
Covered Dish, 8"	$35.00	Plate, deep (Rim Soup), 8"	$8.00
Covered Dish, 9"	$40.00	Plate, deep (Rim Soup), 9"	$9.00
Creamer	$14.00	Salad Bowl	$30.00
Dish (Platter), 6½"	$10.00	Sauce Boat	$20.00
Dish (Platter), 7"	$12.00	Sauce Boat Stand	$26.00
Dish (Platter), 8½"	$13.00	Spoon Holder	$45.00
Dish (Platter), 9½"	$14.50	Sugar, covered	$18.00
Dish (Platter), 10½"	$15.00	Teacup (only)	$5.00
Dish (Platter), 12"	$16.00	Teacup Saucer (only)	$3.50
Dish (Platter), 13½"	$18.00	Teapot	$65.00
Dish (Platter), 14½"	$22.00	Tureen, soup	$60.00
Dish (Platter), 15½"	$25.50	Tureen, soup, Stand	$12.00
Dish (Platter), 16"	$28.00	Tureen, soup, Ladle	$25.00
Dish (Platter), 17"	$30.00	Tureen, sauce	$35.00
Dish (Platter), 19"	$32.00	Tureen, sauce, Stand	$10.00
Fruit, 4"	$4.50	Tureen, sauce, Ladle	$22.00

Plate 252: Catalog picture of pickles, oyster bowl, soup tureen, and soup tureen stand and ladle.

WESTOVER

Westover, dating from 1908, is one of the less ornate shapes of that period. For some unexplained reason, Westover casseroles have proven easy to find. This is true not only of the area around East Liverpool, but on the West Coast as well. Besides casseroles, other serving pieces have turned up in Southern California, although prices are sometimes quite high.

Descriptive points to look for: Westover has no embossing, flat topped handles, and easy-to-recognize finials that are slightly raised in the middle. The flatware pieces are round or oval with smooth edges. While the absence of embossing and other adornments in the body of the piece will certainly rule out some of the other Edwin Knowles shapes, there is no way I know of to positively identify an Edwin Knowles flatware piece as Westover, unless it is found in the company of identifiable hollow ware.

Use Cumberland value guide, page 166.

Plate 253: Westover 100. Casserole with red band segments separated by gold medallions.

Plate 254: The Westover shape from a catalog at the East Liverpool Museum of Ceramics.

Plate 255: Westover 101. Casserole covered with bands of a decal of small pink flowers.

MONTICELLO

This shape dates from 1905 and is another early Edwin Knowles creation. I believe it to be rare. I have only come across one piece but I know there are other pieces just waiting to be found.

Description of points to look for: Monticello has embossing which resembles wheat or grasses tied in the middle. In some places these grasses curl around almost like waves. The same band that ties the grass is repeated on the finials and handles as seen on the teapot and covered dish in Plate 258. The flatware is slightly scalloped.

For a value guide use Mount Vernon, page 159.

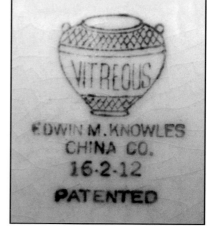

Plate 256: This Edwin Knowles backstamp is found on most early Knowles dinnerware.

Plate 257: Monticello 100. Butter dish with gold decorations.

Plate 258: This is the only catalog-type picture of Monticello dinnerware that I have been able to locate. It was found in the files of the East Liverpool Museum of Ceramics.

MOUNT VERNON

First made in 1909, this shape is shown in an issue of *Glass & Pottery World* of that same year. The outstanding feature of this shape is its attractive use of embossed decorations, particularly on the flatware.

Descriptive points to look for: Mount Vernon has heavy, well-defined embossing (see Plate 260 for a good look at the embossing), round embossed finials, and long looped handles. The flatware has an evenly scalloped rim, the theme of which is repeated on the foot of the hollow ware. Note particularly the embossed ribbon-like loops on each end of the platter.

Value guide page 159.

Plate 259: Vernon 100. Sauce boat, deep plate (rim soup), tea cup and saucer, and sugar with lid covered with garlands of pink roses.

Plate 260: Some pieces of the Mount Vernon shape in an old catalog page from the files of the East Liverpool Museum of Ceramics.

Plate 261: Vernon 101. Casserole with gold stamping around the rim.

MOUNT VERNON

Baker, 6"	$12.00	Fruit, 5"	$6.00
Baker, 7½"	$14.00	Fruit, 6"	$7.00
Baker, 8"	$16.00	Jug, 1 pt.	$25.00
Baker, 9"	$18.00	Jug, 2 pt.	$30.00
Baker, 10"	$22.00	Jug, 3½ pt.	$35.00
Baker, 11"	$24.00	Jug, 4½ pt.	$40.00
Bone Dish	$8.00	Jug, 6 pt.	$50.00
Bowl, deep, 1 pt.	$12.00	Jug, 8 pt.	$65.00
Bowl, deep, 1½ pt.	$14.00	Nappy, 7"	$14.00
Bowl, deep 2 pt.	$13.00	Nappy, 8"	$16.00
Bowl, oyster, 1½ pt.	$12.00	Nappy, 9"	$18.00
Butter, covered	$65.00	Nappy, 10"	$26.00
Butter, individual	$6.50	Nappy, 11"	$24.00
Cake Plate	$25.00	Oatmeal, 6½"	$8.00
Casserole, covered, 8"	$45.00	Pickle	$22.00
Casserole, covered, 9"	$50.00	Plate (Coupe Soup), 7"	$7.00
Casserole, notched	$55.00	Plate (Coupe Soup), 8"	$8.00
Chop Plate	$30.00	Plate (Coupe Soup), 9"	$9.00
Coffee Cup	$12.00	Plate (Coupe Soup), 10"	$12.00
Coffee Saucer	$7.00	Plate, 6"	$5.50
Coffee Saucer, AD	$16.00	Plate, 7"	$7.50
Coffee, AD	$15.00	Plate, 8"	$8.50
Covered Dish, 7½"	$35.00	Plate, 9"	$10.00
Covered Dish, 9"	$40.00	Plate, 10"	$11.00
Covered Dish, 10"	$45.00	Plate, deep (Rim Soup), 9"	$10.00
Cream	$13.00	Ramekin	$10.00
Custard, handled	$18.00	Ramekin, Plate	$4.00
Custard, unhandled	$15.00	Salad Bowl	$30.00
Dish (Platter), 6½"	$10.00	Sauce Boat	$18.00
Dish (Platter), 7"	$11.00	Sauce Boat Stand	$10.00
Dish (Platter), 8½"	$12.00	Sauce Ladle	$22.00
Dish (Platter), 9½"	$13.00	Sauce Tureen Stand	$10.50
Dish (Platter), 10½"	$14.00	Sauce Tureen	$35.00
Dish (Platter), 11½"	$16.00	Spoon Tray	$50.00
Dish (Platter), 12"	$18.00	Sugar	$18.00
Dish (Platter), 13½"	$20.50	Teacup (only)	$6.00
Dish (Platter), 14½"	$24.00	Teacup Saucer (only)	$3.00
Dish (Platter), 16"	$28.00	Teapot	$75.00
Dish (Platter), 17"	$30.00	Tureen Stand	$19.00
Dish (Platter), 19"	$32.00	Tureen, covered	$70.00
Egg Cup, double	$17.50		

Plate 262: Catalog picture of Mt. Vernon.

MAYFLOWER

The Mayflower shape was first brought out in 1914, and was produced at least as late as the 1930s. Due to its long production run, Mayflower is seen often in the antiques market. The shape is characterized by a faceted appearance, which Knowles called "panels." This theme is carried out not only with the hollow ware (note particularly the sauce boat) but also with the flatware, although with a more muted treatment. Except for the panels, the pieces of this shape are otherwise unadorned by embossing of any sort. The shapes of the handles on the hollow ware fall into two different categories. Those on the sauce boat and the cream are almost circular in shape, although the outside of these handles continues the paneled theme. However, as can be seen in Plate 266, the handles of the cups and jugs are rather different, being more ear-shaped. The handles of the casserole are similar to those of the sauce boat stand seen in Plate 263, consisting of flattened loops which are attached so as to continue the lines of the piece.

Value guide page 162.

Plate 263: Mayflower pattern #MF221. Shown are a 12" dish (platter), pickle/sauce boat stand, and sauce boat with pink flowers on a yellow background in a band around the rim.

Plate 264: Mayflower 100. Baker with band of pink flowers separated by shields of gray and blue. Mayflower 101. Covered dish with vivid orange and yellow flowers.

Plate 265: Mayflower 100. Eggcup and butter dish matching baker in Plate 262.

MAYFLOWER

Baker, 5"	$18.00	Egg Cup	$18.00
Baker, 8"	$8.00	Fruit, 5"	$5.00
Baker, 9"	$14.00	Jug, 1 pt.	$20.50
Baker, 10"	$16.00	Jug, 1 pt.	$25.50
Bowl, deep, pt.	$12.00	Jug, 2 pt.	$30.50
Bowl, deep, 1 pt.	$15.50	Jug, 3 pt.	$40.50
Bowl, oyster 1 pt.	$10.00	Jug, 4 pt.	$45.50
Bowl, oyster 1 pt.	$14.00	Nappy, 8"	$16.00
Bouillon	$12.50	Nappy, 9"	$18.00
Bouillon Saucer	$8.00	Nappy, 10"	$20.00
Butter, covered	$55.50	Oatmeal, 6"	$7.00
Butter, individual	$5.00	Pickle	$16.00
Cake Plate	$21.00	Plate (Coupe Soup), 8"	$8.00
Casserole, 8"	$40.00	Plate, 6"	$6.00
Casserole, notched, 9"	$50.00	Plate, 7"	$7.00
Coffee Cup	$12.00	Plate, 8"	$8.00
Coffee Saucer	$6.00	Plate, 9"	$10.00
Covered Dish	$38.00	Plate, 10"	$12.00
Cream	$14.00	Plate, deep (Rim Soup)	$9.00
Cream, individual	$12.00	Sauce Boat	$18.00
Cup, AD	$14.00	Sauce Boat (Fast Stand)	$25.00
Saucer, AD	$6.00	Sauce Boat (Fast Stand, hnld)	$30.00
Custard, footed & handled	$18.00	Sugar, covered	$18.00
Custard, footed	$14.00	Sugar, individual	$14.00
Dish (Platter),11"	$16.00	Teacup (only)	$5.00
Dish (Platter),12"	$18.00	Teacup Saucer (only)	$3.00
Dish (Platter),13"	$21.00	Teapot	$75.00
Dish (Platter),15"	$22.50	Teapot, individual	$45.00
Dish (Platter), well, 17"	$28.00	Teapot Tile	$20.00

Plate 266: Catalog pictures of Mayflower.

1	Bakers	13	Cream	25	Plates
2	Cake Plate	14	Cream, individual	26	Rim Soup
3	Bowl, deep	15	Custard, footed & handled	27	Coupe Soup
4	Bowl, oyster	16	Custard, footed	28	Sauce Boat
5	Bouillon	17	Dishes (Platters)	29	Sauce Boat, Fast Stand
6	Butter, covered	18	Dish (Platter) Well	30	Sugar
7	Butter, individual	19	Egg Cup	31	Sugar, individual
8	Casserole	20	Fruit	32	Teapot
9	Casserole, notched	21	Jugs	33	Teapot, individual
10	Coffee Cup	22	Nappies	34	Teapot Tile
11	Coffee, A.D.	23	Oatmeal	35	Teacup
12	Covered Dish	24	Pickle		

HAMPTON

The Hampton shape dates from 1914 and is shown in the 1925 Butler Brothers catalog with the Blue Bird pattern, a decoration highly prized by collectors today. The span of 11 years between the date of its introduction and its appearance in the Butler Brothers mail-order catalog would imply a reasonably long production lifetime. Nevertheless, this shape has been difficult to locate. The sugar pictured below is the only piece I have been able to locate so far.

Descriptive points to look for: Hampton has no embossing. Finials are simple, arched shapes. Handles on the casseroles are vertical instead of horizontal. The most distinctive feature of this shape is its solid-looking foot and slightly plump shape. The flatware of the Hampton shape is round or oval with smooth edges, with little else to distinguish it. This observation, it must be added, is based only on the old catalog page pictured below, since I have not had an opportunity to personally see or handle any of the flatware.

Value guide page 165.

Plate 267: Hampton 100. The backstamp on this sugar dates it as 1922.

Plate 268: Pieces of Hampton from a catalog at the East Liverpool Museum of Ceramics.

1	Bakers	19	Plates
2	Cake Plate	20	Jugs
3	Bowls, deep	21	Nappies
4	Bowls, oyster	22	Plate
5	Bouillon	28	Sauce Boat
8	Casserole	29	Sauce Boat, Fast Stand
9	Casserole, notched	31	Sugar
10	Coffee	34	Teacup
14	Cream	36	Ladle
17	Dishes (Platters)		

HAMPTON

Baker, 5"	$10.00	Egg Cup, double	$15.50
Baker, 6"	$12.00	Fruit, 5"	$5.00
Baker, 7"	$14.00	Fruit, 6"	$6.00
Baker, 8"	$16.00	Jug, pt.	$16.00
Baker, 9"	$18.00	Jug, 1 pt.	$20.00
Baker, 10"	$20.00	Jug, 1 pt.	$25.00
Baker, 11"	$22.00	Jug, 2 pt.	$30.00
Bone Dish	$8.00	Jug, 3 pt.	$35.00
Bouillon	$12.00	Jug, 4 pt.	$40.00
Bouillon Saucer	$6.00	Jug, 6 pt.	$45.00
Bowl, deep, 1 pt.	$12.00	Nappy, 6"	$12.00
Bowl, deep, 1½ pt.	$14.00	Nappy, 7"	$16.00
Bowl, oyster, 1½ pt.	$10.00	Nappy, 8"	$18.00
Bowl, oyster, 1 pt.	$12.00	Nappy, 9"	$20.00
Butter, covered	$50.00	Nappy, 10"	$22.00
Butter, individual	$5.50	Oatmeal, 6"	$7.00
Cake Plate	$20.00	Pickle	$18.00
Casserole, covered, 8"	$35.00	Plate (Coupe Soup), 7"	$8.00
Casserole, notched cover, 9"	$40.00	Plate (Coupe Soup), 8"	$9.00
Chop Plate	$25.00	Plate (Coupe Soup), 9"	$12.00
Coffee Cup	$12.00	Plate, 6"	$4.50
Coffee Saucer	$7.00	Plate, 7"	$5.50
Coffee Saucer, AD	$6.00	Plate, 8"	$8.50
Coffee, AD	$16.00	Plate, 9"	$9.00
Covered Dish, 7"	$30.00	Plate, 10"	$10.00
Covered Dish, 9"	$35.00	Plate, deep (Rim Soup), 6"	$7.00
Creamer	$12.00	Plate, deep (Rim Soup), 9"	$9.00
Custard, handled	$16.00	Sauce Boat	$18.00
Custard, unhandled	$14.00	Sauce Boat (Fast Stand)	$24.00
Dish (Platter), 7"	$11.00	Sauce Ladle	$22.00
Dish (Platter), 8"	$12.00	Sauce Tureen Stand	$10.50
Dish (Platter), 9"	$13.00	Sauce Tureen	$30.00
Dish (Platter), 10"	$14.00	Soup Ladle	$25.00
Dish (Platter), 11"	$15.00	Sugar	$18.00
Dish (Platter), 12"	$16.00	Teacup (only)	$5.00
Dish (Platter), 13"	$17.50	Teacup Saucer (only)	$3.00
Dish (Platter), 14"	$19.00	Teapot	$65.00
Dish (Platter), 15"	$20.00	Teapot, individual	$35.00
Dish (Platter), 17"	$24.00		

WESTOVER and CUMBERLAND

Baker, 5"	$10.00	Fruit, 5"	$5.00
Baker, 6"	$12.00	Fruit, 5"	$6.00
Baker, 8"	$14.00	Fruit, 6"	$7.00
Baker, 9"	$16.00	Jug, pt.	$16.00
Baker, 10"	$18.00	Jug, 1 pt.	$20.00
Baker, 11"	$20.00	Jug, 1 pt.	$25.00
Bone Dish	$6.00	Jug, 2 pt.	$30.00
Bouillon	$12.00	Jug, 3 pt.	$35.00
Bouillon Saucer	$6.00	Jug, 4 pt.	$40.00
Bowl, deep, 1 pt.	$12.00	Jug, 5 pt.	$45.00
Bowl, deep, 1½ pt.	$14.00	Ladle	$22.00
Bowl, oyster, 1 pt.	$10.00	Nappy, 7"	$12.00
Bowl, oyster, 1½ pt.	$12.00	Nappy, 8"	$16.00
Butter, covered	$50.00	Nappy, 9"	$18.00
Butter, individual	$5.50	Nappy, 10"	$20.00
Cake Plate	$25.00	Nappy, 11"	$22.00
Casserole, covered, 8"	$40.00	Oatmeal, 6"	$7.00
Casserole, covered, 9"	$45.00	Pickle	$18.00
Chop Plate	$25.00	Plate (Coupe Soup), 7"	$8.00
Coffee Cup	$12.00	Plate (Coupe Soup), 10"	$9.00
Coffee Saucer	$7.00	Plate, 6"	$4.50
Coffee Saucer, AD	$6.00	Plate, 7"	$5.50
Coffee, AD	$14.00	Plate, 8"	$8.50
Covered Dish, 7"	$30.00	Plate, 9"	$9.00
Covered Dish, 8"	$35.00	Plate, 10"	$10.00
Covered Dish, 9"	$40.00	Plate, deep (Rim Soup), 6"	$7.00
Cream	$12.00	Plate, deep (Rim Soup), 8"	$8.00
Custard, handled	$18.00	Plate, deep (Rim Soup), 9"	$9.00
Custard, unhandled	$15.00	Ramekin	$9.00
Dish (Platter), 7"	$11.00	Ramekin, Plate	$4.00
Dish (Platter), 8"	$12.00	Salad Bowl	$25.00
Dish (Platter), 9"	$13.00	Sauce Boat	$18.00
Dish (Platter), 10"	$14.00	Sauce Boat (Fast Stand)	$25.00
Dish (Platter), 11"	$15.00	Sauce Boat Stand	$9.00
Dish (Platter), 12"	$16.00	Sauce Ladle	$22.00
Dish (Platter), 13"	$17.50	Sauce Tureen Stand	$10.50
Dish (Platter), 14"	$19.00	Sauce Tureen	$35.00
Dish (Platter), 15"	$20.00	Spoon Tray	$40.00
Dish (Platter), 16"	$22.00	Sugar	$18.00
Dish (Platter), 17"	$24.00	Teacup (only)	$5.00
Dish (Platter), 18"	$26.00	Teacup Saucer (only)	$3.00
Dish (Platter), 20"	$28.00	Teapot	$65.00
Egg Cup, double	$16.50	Tureen Stand	$15.00
Fruit, 4"	$4.00	Tureen, covered	$55.00

CUMBERLAND

Dating from 1915, the Cumberland shape is easy to confuse with the very similar Hampton shape on page 164. Although not plentiful, Cumberland has certainly proven easier to find than Hampton. Besides the pieces shown below, I have been successful in finding an entire set of Cumberland, surprisingly from a local dealer in Southern California.

Descriptive points to look for: Cumberland has no embossing. The flatware pieces are round or oval with smooth edges. Finials are simple curved arches, but are slightly longer and higher than Hampton. Note that Cumberland hollow ware has a sturdy foot but a taller and slightly less rounded look than Hampton.

Value guide page 166.

Plate 269: Cumberland 100. This fast stand sauce boat and casserole have bands of pink flowers on yellow, which are the same decoration as seen on the Mayflower shape on page 161, Plate 261. Here again is evidence that potters would use the same decal on different shapes.

Plate 270: The Cumberland shape from a catalog at the East Liverpool Museum of Ceramics.

1	Bakers	17	Dishes (Platters)
2	Cake Plate	20	Jugs
3	Bowls, deep	21	Nappies
4	Bowls, oyster	22	Oatmeal
5	Bouillon	28	Sauce Boat
6	Covered Dish	29	Sauce Boat, Fast Stand
9	Tureen, covered	31	Sugar
10	Coffee Cup	34	Teacup
14	Cream	36	Ladle

SPECIALTIES

Like most pottery companies, Edwin Knowles made various special items which can be found in antiques stores today. On the next page in Plate 274 is a catalog picture showing some of these.

Plate 271: Ohio Jugs. These jugs, with their art deco decoration and unusual handles and knobs, are perhaps my own personal favorites. They are, fortunately, easy to find. These jugs are shown in a 1909 copy of *Glass and Pottery World* along with an article which reads "The Edwin M. Knowles China Co., E. Liverpool, O., are adding several new shapes and patterns to their long lines of covered jugs. They are almost alone in this field." This article was a bit misleading. Many other potteries of that time made their own type of "Ohio" jug. These jugs are often seen in batter sets.

Plate 272: Colonial creamer. The medallion on this small specialty creamer is reminiscent of a religious medal.

Plate 273: Five-pint Chester jug with a floral decal.

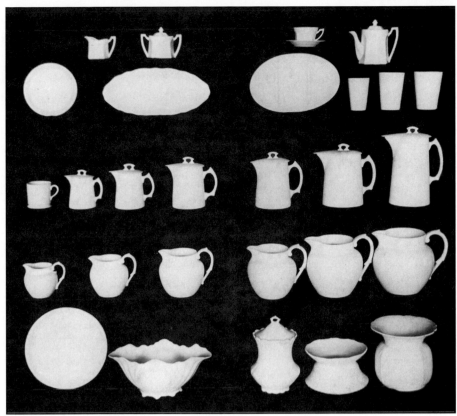

Plate 274: Edwin Knowles specialties from a catalog at the East Liverpool Museum of Ceramics.

SPECIALTIES

Baby Plates	$45.00	Jug, Ohio, covered, 2 pt.	$40.50
Celery Tray	$25.00	Jug, Ohio, covered, 3 pt.	$45.50
Cheese Tray	$18.00	Jug, Ohio, covered, 4 pt.	$55.50
Cheese Cover	$50.00	Muffin, covered	$45.00
Cream Soup	$16.00	Mug, Baltimore	$16.00
Cream Soup, Saucer	$6.00	Mug, Ohio, 7 oz.	$15.00
Creamer, colonial	$15.50	Mug, Ohio, 12 oz.	$18.00
Cracker Jar	$45.00	Mug, soda, 14 oz.	$20.00
Compartment Tray, oval	$35.00	Mug, child's, 9 oz.	$16.00
Compartment Tray, round	$30.00	Orange Bowls	$55.00
Covered (Baking) Dish, 7"	$25.00	Plaque, 8"	$20.00
Covered (Baking) Dish, 8"	$30.00	Plaque, 9"	$25.00
Guest Room Tray	$35.00	Salad Bowl, octagonal	$25.00
Jug, Chester, 1 pt.	$20.00	Salad Plate, plain	$12.00
Jug, Chester, 1½ pt.	$25.00	Salad Plate, embossed	$18.00
Jug, Chester, 2½ pt.	$30.00	Service Plate, octagonal	$25.00
Jug, Chester, 3 pt.	$35.00	Sugar, colonial	$20.00
Jug, Chester, 5 pt.	$45.00	Tea Cup, colonial	$10.00
Jug, Chester, 6 pt.	$50.00	Tea Saucer, colonial	$4.00
Jug, Ohio, covered, 1 pt.	$25.00	Teapot, colonial	$75.00
Jug, Ohio, covered, 1 pt.	$30.50	Compartment Baker	$20.00

The D.E. McNicol Pottery Company
East Liverpool, Ohio & Clarksburg, West Virginia

The D.E. McNicol Pottery Company was founded in East Liverpool, Ohio, in 1892, when the former McNicol, Burton, and Company was incorporated and Daniel McNicol assumed control as its president. The company made semivitreous dinnerware, toilet wares, and other ceramic wares. The company was unusual in that it seems to have continued to focus significant energies on the making of yellow ware, a practice largely abandoned by other china makers of the area. In 1914, the company built a plant in Clarksburg, West Virginia. In 1919, another plant was opened in East Liverpool, making a total of four. Eventually all of the East Liverpool operations were terminated, and the company continued operation in Clarksburg, making hotel wares. The company was still in operation in 1960.

Nothing in the American chinaware business seems simple, and the McNicol story is certainly no exception. Another pottery, T.A. McNicol, was founded by one of Daniel's sons, Thomas, who took over the defunct Globe China Company in 1913. This company used a different backstamp, and should therefore not be confused with the D.E. McNicol operation.

During the period of time which is the focus of this book, the D.E. McNicol China Company produced semivitreous porcelain dinnerware products from their East Liverpool operation. They also produced calendar and commemorative plates, a surprisingly large number of which have survived to the present day.

Value guide page 178.

Plate 275: A picture of the D.E. McNicol Pottery, dated Aug. 4, 1902, from the East Liverpool Museum of Ceramics.

Plate 276: Colonial shape.

Plate 277: Ursula shape. These pictures from the 1902 *China, Glass & Lamps*, a china trade magazine, are of old D.E. McNicol dinnerware. The embossing, handles, and finials shown in these pictures should help with the identification of this shape.

IDEAL

Gates and Ormerod[1] date the Ideal backstamp as ca. 1905. The platter shown below in Plate 278 was the only result of a 6-month search for this shape in antiques shops and flea markets in West Virginia. I think it is safe to say that Ideal is a rare shape.

Description of points to look for: Ideal has no embossing. The hollow ware has simple loop handles and knobs. The flatware has a smooth edge and wide rims. This graceful and very simple shape made a perfect background for the popular Blue Bird pattern shown in Plate 279.

Value guide page 178.

Plate 278: Ideal 100. Ideal platter with large roses.

Plates 279 and 280: From a McNicol advertising booklet found at the East Liverpool Museum of Ceramics, dated 1919 – 1920.

OHIO

The Ohio backstamp, shown in Plate 282, is dated by Gates and Ormerod as ca. 1915 to 1925. Ohio was found both in sets and individual pieces. The pieces in my own collection were found in different areas of the eastern U.S.

Description of points to look for: The Ohio shape has flatware similar to the Carnation shape (see page 175) but with a different, lighter embossing. A close up of the embossing is shown in Plate 283. The scalloped edge of the flatware is slightly more irregular than Carnation but you still must look closely to tell the difference between the two. The hollow ware has a flat triangular finial and large smoothly shaped handles.

Value guide page 178.

Plate 281: Ohio 100. 11" dish (platter), 10" plate, coupe soup, and fruit with decal of red and yellow roses in center and gold stamping on the edge.

Plate 282: Backstamp found on Ohio dishes.

Plate 283: Embossing found on the Ohio shape.

Plate 284: Ohio 102. 10" plate may be a specialty plate or part of a dinnerware set.

Plate 285: The Ohio shape is shown in a booklet put out by the D.E. McNicol Company. [From the East Liverpool Museum of Ceramics.]

Plate 286: Ohio 102. Large jug with a beautiful flower decal.

CARNATION

Carnation is one of the more easily found McNicol shapes. Not only is it easy to find, but all the pieces I have seen were beautifully decorated, thus making it well worth collecting.

Description of points to look for: The Carnation shape is easy to identify because of the scalloped embossing that circles its rim. The casserole finial and handles are long flat ovals, which also show a scalloped embossing and are very solidly attached to the body. The flatware edges have a very even, rounded scallop.

Value guide page 178.

Plate 287: Carnation 100. Casserole with pink flowers. Carnation 101. 10" plate with orange glaze on the rim and flowers in the center.

Plate 288: McNicol backstamp from the pink plate on the left in Plate 291.
Plate 289: McNicol backstamp from the orange plate on the right in Plate 291.

Plate 290: Close-up of embossing on the Carnation shape.

Plate 291: Carnation 101 (left). Carnation 102 (right). These plates may have been made as specialty plates or as part of a regular dinnerware set. Even though they are identical except for color, they each carry a different backstamp. The pink plate on the left, has the Carnation backstamp as shown in Plate 288, which indicated it was made in East Liverpool, while the orange plate on the right, with the backstamp in Plate 289, was made in Clarksburg.

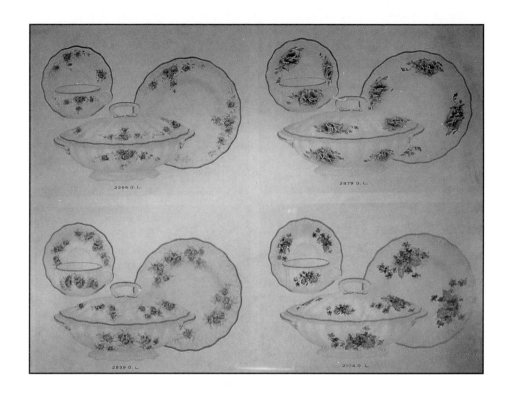

Plates 292 and 293:
Some of the Carnation shapes shown in a booklet found at the East Liverpool of Ceramics.

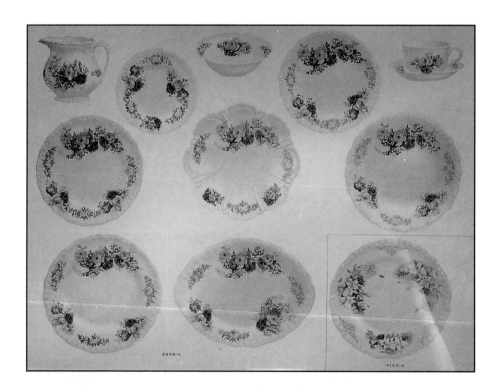

IDEAL, OHIO, CARNATION & LAUREL

Baker, 6"	$6.00	Jug, 2½ pt.	$30.00
Baker, 8"	$14.00	Jug, 4 pt.	$40.00
Baker, 9"	$16.50	Jug, 5½ pt.	$45.00
Baker, 10"	$18.00	Nappy, 7"	$14.00
Berry Saucer, 6"	$8.00	Nappy, 8"	$16.00
Bone Dish	$8.00	Nappy, 9"	$18.00
Bowl, deep	$12.50	Nappy, 10"	$20.00
Butter, covered	$55.00	Oatmeal, 6"	$6.00
Butter, individual	$5.00	Pickle	$16.50
Casserole, covered	$40.00	Plate (Coupe Soup), 8"	$8.00
Casserole, notched	$45.00	Plate (Coupe Soup), 9"	$9.00
Coffee Cup	$10.00	Plate, 6"	$5.00
Coffee Saucer	$6.00	Plate, 7"	$6.00
Coffee Saucer, AD	$6.00	Plate, 8"	$7.50
Covered Dish, 8"	$35.00	Plate, 9"	$9.00
Covered Dish, 9"	$40.00	Plate, 10"	$10.00
Cream	$13.50	Plate, deep (Rim Soup), 8"	$9.00
Dish (Platter), 11½"	$18.00	Plate, deep (Rim Soup), 9"	$10.00
Dish (Platter), 13½"	$20.00	Sauce Boat	$18.50
Dish (Platter), 15½"	$24.00	Sauce Boat (Fast Stand)	$24.00
Dish (Platter), 17½"	$28.00	Sugar, covered	$18.00
Fruit, 5"	$5.00	Teacup (only)	$5.00
Fruit, 6"	$6.00	Teacup Saucer (only)	$3.00
Jug, ¾ pt.	$16.00	Teapot	$65.00
Jug, 1 pt.	$20.00	Tureen	$60.00
Jug, 1¾ pt.	$25.00		

LAUREL

As noted below, the Laurel shape is shown in a 1919 advertising booklet put out by D.E. McNicol. So far that is the only date located for this shape, which should be considered rare but not impossible to find.

Description of points to look for: Laurel has no embossing. It has a round, flat, button-like knob and flat-topped handles easily seen in Plates 295 and 296. The hollow ware has smooth edges and is round or oval.

Value guide above.

Plate 294: Laurel 100. Sauce boat and sauce boat stand.

Plate 295: The Laurel shape, from a small advertising booklet photographed at the East Liverpool Museum of Ceramics, dated 1919 to 1920.

Plate 296: Laurel 101. Teapot and creamer done with a very striking pink glaze, offset with black. I was outbid at the Sells Auction house in Wellsville for this set but was later able to photograph it thanks to its new owners, Bill and Donna Gray of Maryland.

McNICOL SPECIALTY ITEMS

D.E. McNicol was well known for their specialty items.
Listed below is a value guide of a few of those items.

Calendar, Advertising, or Specialty Plate	$18.00 – 28.00
Salad Bowl	$15.00 – 20.00
Cake Plate	$20.00 – 30.00
Child's Plate with Metal Holder	$85.00 – 95.00

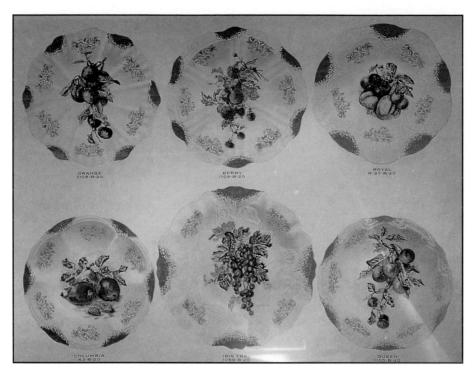

Plate 297: Cake plates and salad bowl from a catalog at the East Liverpool Ceramics Museum.

Plate 298: Deep salad bowls in the Ohio shape and Swiss salad bowls in the Carnation shape. Picture from a catalog at the East Liverpool Ceramics Museum.

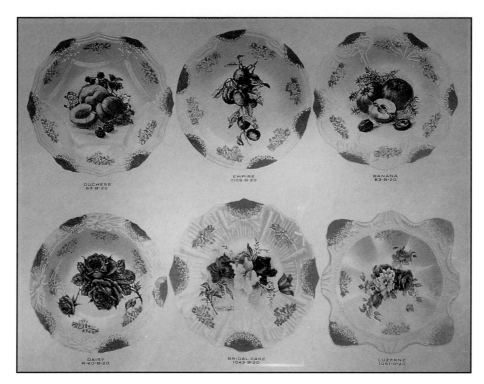

Plate 299: Salad bowls and cake plates from a catalog at the East Liverpool Museum of Ceramics.

Plate 300: McNicol 100. These two plates were part of a set showing cartoons of Dutch children. Each plate has a different cartoon, below which appears a remark or saying in a mockingly heavy Dutch accent.

Plate 301: McNicol 101. Fasthold baby plate. This one is without the special metal piece that attached the plate to either a table or highchair.

Plate 302: Advertising plates, McNicol 102, on left with pheasants; and McNicol 103, on the right with apples.

All of the plates shown above are from the collection of Donna and Bill Gray of Columbia, Maryland. For value guide, see page 179.

Mercer Pottery

The Mercer Pottery Company was located in Trenton, New Jersey, a region that competed with the East Liverpool District as a china-making center. Mercer began operation in 1868, and operated until the 1930s. From an article out of the *Crockery & Glass Journal* dated 1876 we read:

> The works of the Mercer Pottery Company…are of the largest in Trenton and recently passed into the hands of Mr. James Moses…they are situated on Railroad Ave. in close proximity to the Delaware and Raitain Canal, and directly upon the Belvidero Railroad. The main building is of stone, two and one half stories high. The kiln sheds, bisque warerooms, and sagger shops form a building 50 by 288 feet, while the wareroom for finished stock is two and a half stories in height. The different departments are all so arranged that the raw material enters at the rear of the establishment, and passing through one process to another directly towards the front, reaches the main building. An inspection therefore begun at the office, encounters piles of glossy finished ware.
>
> At the Mercer pottery we found a decorating room of large dimensions on one side of which was stored the completed work, glistening with gilt and beautiful with colors. Next we saw the ware as it had left the kilns, still unpolished and black from the effects of the heat or liquid gold. At the other end sat the decorators — many of them girls — hard at work with paint, gold, and brushes. They are adepts at their trade, and turn out work with astonishing rapidity and perfection. The gilt to be seen upon ware is the purest gold, being reduced to a liquid by means of acid. It is then applied by a camel's hair pencil, as is also the most delicate tint, and when the design is fully executed, the ware is burned, then polished by means of burnishers.
>
> The capacity of the works is upwards of $175,000 worth of white granite and C.C. ware per annum. The works are operated by steam, generated by a boiler of sixty-horse power. The engine is a Corliss, thirty-horse power, and one of the best of that most excellent of inventions.
>
> The company employs a force numbering about 120, a large number being from the best English potteries. The success of the establishment is undoubtedly due to the superior ability evinced by the proprietor and manager, Mr. James Moses. For a long time he was connected with the Glasgow pottery, of this city.

The examples of Mercer wares that I have found on the antiques market have proven to be of a very high quality. I have, not surprisingly, found Mercer in New Jersey. I have also found it in the East Liverpool area, which seems rather like carrying coals to Newcastle. I have also found it in California, a long way from its home in the east. Not only have I found individual pieces, but I have also encountered a complete dinnerware set in New Jersey and most recently in Sacramento, California. Thus the collector of Mercer will find their excursions to the antiques shops and flea markets well rewarded. However, as can be seen by the examples shown on the following pages, it is easy to overlook older examples of Mercer, as they strongly resemble English china. I answered an advertisement for a Mercer "English" teapot which, as I expected, was really "American" and made by Mercer in New Jersey.

Plate 303: Pictures from *China, Glass and Lamps* magazine dated 1900. These show two very similar casseroles in the white granite ware that was typical of that time. The casserole on the left is the Berlin shape and on the right is the Vienna shape.

Plate 304: Berlin 100. Tureen from the collection of Frederick Morth of Rehoboth, Massachusetts.

BELMONT

As the advertisement here shows, Mercer made a square shape called Belmont.

For a value guide for Belmont and the dishes on page 185 see page 191.

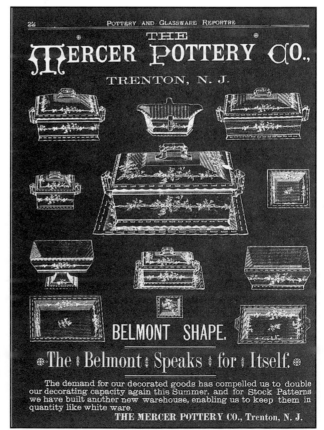

Plate 305: Advertisement from the *Pottery and Glassware Reporter* dated 1880. I found this picture in Minnie Kamm's *Old China*[4].

Plate 306: Mercer 100. Square tureen and ladle with brown transfer style decoration.

Plate 307: Mercer 101. Teapot, which also has the familiar brown transfer style decoration.

LOWESTOFT

The only date I was able to find for this intriguing shape was from an advertisement in the September 9, 1926 *Pottery, Glass & Brass Salesman* trade magazine. The most important feature of Lowestoft are the rope-like handles and the intermittent gadroon or rope-like embossed edge on the plate, interspersed with sections clean of embossing, as pictured in Plate 310. The knob type of finial on the sugar repeats the rope look. The sugar and creamer stand on three little feet.

For value guide see page 191.

Left:
Plate 308: Mercer backstamp dating from 1890.

Right:
Plate 309: Mercer backstamp dating from 1928.

MERCER LOWESTOFT

Buyers visiting New York are cordially invited to inspect our New Display Room at 200 Fifth Avenue, Room No. 356.

UNDER-GLAZE DECORATIONS — LOWESTOFT SHAPE IVORY BODY. UNDER-GLAZE DECORATED HOTEL WARE.

OVER-GLAZE DECORATED DINNERWARE WHITE BODY.

"Lowestoft Old Bouquet Design Under-Glaze"

MERCER POTTERY COMPANY
Trenton, New Jersey

Agent: E. M. Meder Co.
17 North Wabash Avenue, Chicago

Agent: Frank C. Branum
252 Wilcox Building, Los Angeles, Cal.

Plate 310: Advertisement from September 9, 1926, *Pottery, Glass & Brass Salesman.*

Plate 311: Lowestoft 100. Sugar and creamer with band of bright orange and blue flowers.

OTHER MERCER DINNERWARE

Unfortunately, information allowing the identification of Mercer shapes is sadly lacking. While the Ohio State Historical Society has taken great pains to preserve its heritage of potting in the East Liverpool Museum of Ceramics, the same cannot be said for the New Jersey area. The Mercer shapes shown below undoubtedly had names as well as catalog pages showing all of the different pieces. None of this information has yet come to light, so the best that can be done is to show the wares themselves, allowing the readers to speculate about what these shapes were originally called.

Here is a shape that would gladden the heart of any collector of early American dinnerware. From its decoration and its overall design, I would place it at some time between 1900 and 1920.

Description of points to look for: The ornate finials (see Plate 312 for a good look at the finial) are its most distinctive feature. The areas under the finials and the handle are embossed. The solid foot on the hollow ware is scalloped, as are the edges of the flatware.

For suggested values see page 191.

Plate 312: Mercer 102. Covered dish with wide bands in blue and white.

Plate 313: Mercer 103. 10" plate, cup, and saucer with a band of pink flowers.

Plate 314: Mercer 103. Covered dish in the same pattern as dishes in Plate 311.

Plate 315: Mercer 103. A sugar without its lid and a handled custard.

Plate 316: Mercer 103. Sauce boat.

A large set of this unidentified shape was located in the New Jersey area (see Plates 318 and 319). Another was found in California (see Plate 317). The backstamps on these sets (see page 186 for a picture of the backstamps) provide a date of around 1928.

Description of points to look for: This shape has no embossing. The finial on the covered dish (see Plate 318) is a simple arch style but the finial on the butter dish (see Plate 317) is a very definite oval. The handle on the sauce boat has a pointy-ear look. The flatware is round or oval with smooth edges.

Value guide on page 191.

Plate 317: Mercer 104. 11" dish (platter), creamer, cup and saucer, and butter dish decorated with a band of dark blue flowers, red flowers, and brown leaves.

Plate 318: Mercer 105. Fruit, covered dish, cup, and saucer with bands of blue and flower inserts.

Plate 319: Mercer 105. 15" dish (platter), 8" plate, and sauce boat.

MERCER

Baker, 8"...........................$14.00 – 18.00	Jug, 3 pt. ....$35.00 – 45.00
Baker, 9"...........................$16.00 – 20.00	Jug, 5 pt. ....$40.00 – 55.00
Baker, 10"..........................$18.00 – 24.00	Nappy, 8".........................$14.00 – 18.00
Bone Dish...........................$6.00 – 8.00	Nappy, 9".........................$16.00 – 20.00
Bowl, deep, 1 pt...................$10.00 – 14.00	Nappy, 10".......................$18.00 – 24.00
Bowl, deep, 1½ pt. ....$12.00 – 16.00	Oatmeal.............................$6.00 – 8.00
Butter, covered ....$40.00 – 55.00	Pickle ....$14.00 – 24.00
Butter, individual ....$4.50 – 6.00	Plate (Coupe Soup),...................$7.00 – 9.00
Casserole, covered.................$40.00 – 55.00	Plate, 6"...........................$4.50 – 6.00
Coffee Cup ....$8.00 – 10.00	Plate, 7"...........................$5.50 – 7.00
Coffee Saucer ....$5.00 – 7.00	Plate, 8"...........................$7.00 – 8.50
Coffee Saucer, AD...................$5.00 – 7.00	Plate, 9"...........................$8.00 – 10.00
Coffee Cup, AD ....$13.00 – 16.00	Plate, 10".........................$10.00 – 12.00
Comport ....$55.00 – 75.00	Plate, deep (Rim Soup) ....$8.00 – 10.00
Covered Dish ....$35.00 – 50.00	Ramekin...........................$10.00 – 14.00
Cream................................$12.00 – 14.00	Ramekin Saucer.......................$4.00 – 6.00
Custard, handled...................$14.00 – 18.00	Sauce Boat ....$18.00 – 22.00
Custard, unhandled...............$12.00 – 14.00	Sauce Boat (Fast Stand) ....$22.50 – 25.00
Dish (Platter), 8" ....$10.00 – 12.00	Sauce Boat Stand ....$8.00 – 10.00
Dish (Platter), 9" ....$12.00 – 14.00	Sauce Tureen ....$35.00 – 40.00
Dish (Platter), 11" ....$14.00 – 16.00	Sauce Tureen, Stand ....$10.00 – 12.00
Dish (Platter), 13" ....$16.00 – 18.00	Sauce Tureen, Ladle ....$22.00 – 24.00
Dish (Platter), 15" ....$20.00 – 24.00	Sugar, covered ....$16.00 – 18.00
Dish (Platter), 17" ....$24.00 – 28.00	Teacup (only) ....$5.00 – 7.00
Dish (Platter), 19" ....$26.00 – 32.00	Teacup Saucer (only) ....$2.50 – 4.00
Egg Cup ....$15.50 – 18.00	Teapot................................$55.00 – 75.00
Fruit ....$4.00 – 6.00	Tureen, soup ....$55.00 – 80.00
Jug, pt. ....$18.00 – 22.00	Tureen, soup, Ladle ....$24.00 – 26.00
Jug, 1 pt. ....$22.00 – 25.00	

Pope-Gosser China Company

Located outside the East Liverpool District in Coshocton, Ohio, the company was organized in 1902 by Charles F. Gosser and Bentley Pope. Pope was a skillful decorator who was born in England. He came to America in 1870, and worked at Trenton until 1891, when he moved to Ohio. At that time he became manager of KTK until 1903, when he left to form the Pope-Gosser China Company with Gosser. The wares were "excellently potted" (Lehner[3]) and the shapes were a departure from existing models. The company immediately began to produce high grade translucent china for vases, etc. Not finding profit in this line, the company switched to dinnerware which was harder than the usual dinnerware of the times.

Pope-Gosser joined the ill-fated American China Company in 1929. After the demise of that company, Pope-Gosser was reorganized in 1932 by Frank Judge. The company continued to make semiporcelain wares until 1958, although the quality of these wares was not up to the standards of the old company.

Wares from Pope-Gosser are frequently found in antiques shops, although the more recent products predominate. Within the period covered by this book, Pope-Gosser made two noteworthy dinnerware shapes: Louvre (which was another attempt by American potters to imitate the works of Haviland of France) and Edgemore. Of these two, the Edgemore shape has shown up quite often, even in shops in the Southern California area. Perhaps this is due to its rather unusual (but quite attractive) appearance, which makes it easy to spot even when it is mingled in with shapes by other potters. If you have not yet encountered Pope-Gosser's Edgemore dinnerware, do not hesitate to pick up a piece and examine it next time you find it. Note the workmanship and the feeling of delicacy that make it stand out from the wares of other potters of the same time and region.

Plate 320: Pope-Gosser backstamp.

Plate 321: Pope-Gosser 100. Plate with special decal of a rabbit in the winter snow. Not surprisingly this decal was spotted on a Harker plate. It has long been known that different potteries often obtained decals from a common outside source.

Plate 322: Picture of Pope-Gosser pottery from the East Liverpool Museum of Ceramics.

Specialty or Advertising plates ....$25.00 – 35.00

LOUVRE

The Pope Gosser catalogs showing Louvre and Edgemore were found, strangely enough, in the historical files of the Homer Laughlin China Company. The catalog showing the Louvre shape unfortunately had no date. Louvre also appears in the *China, Glass, and Lamps* trade magazine in 1909 and 1911, thus giving some opportunity to establish production dates. It is also shown in the Montgomery Wards catalog in 1915. Wards shows a "yellow Roman Gold band set," a pattern which brings out the gold on the embossing. We see it again in the 1925 Butler Bros. catalog, in an all-white pattern which they called New Louvre.

Description of points to look for: This is Pope-Gosser's imitation of a similar Haviland shape. Value guide page 198.

Plate 323: Louvre 100. Fast stand sauce boat with gold band and gold stamping. New Louvre. 9" baker in all white.

Plate 324: Catalog picture of Louvre from the collection at the Homer Laughlin China Co.

1	Teacup and Saucer	10	Bowl, deep
2	Bouillon & Saucer	11	Oatmeal
3	Fruit	12	Sauce Boat, Fast Stand
4	Butter, individual	13	Butter, covered
5	A.D. Coffee & Saucer	14	Bone Dish
6	Chocolate Cup & Saucer	15	Baker showing foot
7	Coffee Cup & Saucer	16	Dish (Platter) showing foot
8	Sugar	17	Nappy
9	Cream	18	Pickle

19	Plate
20	Dish (Platter)
21	Baker
22	Coupe Soup
23	Covered Dish
24	Soup Tureen
25	Jug
26	Casserole

EDGEMORE

The Edgemore shape is shown in the 1918 Montgomery Wards catalog in the Julia pattern (see page 197, Plate 329 for picture of Julia). It also appears in the 1925 Butler Brothers catalog in Admiral (a pattern of white with gold hair lines), Gold Medallion (an appropriate name, since it has gold stamped medallions), Honeymoon (with delft-blue border decorations), Edgemore (bands of pink rose clusters between gray dotted lines), and Deluxe (a pattern in white with coin-gold bands). While no specific date for the start of Edgemore production has been established, it can probably be dated after Louvre based on its style.

Description of points to look for: The hollow ware has a distinctive shape, resembling two flattened cones joined at the wide ends. Lids on hollow ware pieces, like the sugar, maintain this basic form almost as though the lid and body were formed as one piece and the lid separated afterward. The finials are simple loops, while the handles are large circles oriented vertically. Embossing would only detract from the impact of the basic shape, and indeed, these wares have no embossing at all. Flatware, in both round and oval shapes, is also without embossing. Pick up a piece of Edgemore and note its light and elegant feel.

Value guide page 198.

Plate 325: Edgemore 100. 10" plate and nappy with exotic bird decal.

Plate 326: Edgemore 101. Sugar and creamer with a border of red and gold.

Plate 327: Edgemore 102. 10" plate and sugar with border of fruit and orange flowers on tan.

Plate 328: Edgemore 103. 10" plate, cream soup, and cream soup saucer.

Plate 329: Julia Pink Rose. Sauce boat and casserole.

Plate 330: Edgemore 104. A 10" plate decorated with blue birds.

LOUVRE and EDGEMORE

(L: Louvre only, E: Edgemore only)

	Baker, 5"	$9.50
L	Baker, 7"	$12.00
L	Baker, 8"	$14.00
	Baker, 9"	$16.50
	Baker, 10"	$18.00
	Bone Dish, footed	$6.00
	Bouillon Cup	$12.00
	Bouillon Saucer	$6.00
	Bowl, deep, 36	$12.00
	Bowl, deep, 30	$14.00
	Butter, covered	$55.00
	Butter, individual	$5.00
	Cake Plate	$25.00
	Casserole, covered	$45.00
	Casserole, notched	$50.00
	Chocolate Cup	$14.00
	Chocolate Saucer	$6.50
	Coffee Cup	$10.00
	Coffee Saucer	$6.00
	Coffee Saucer, AD	$6.00
	Coffee, AD	$16.00
	Covered Dish, 9"	$40.00
	Creamer	$13.50
	Creamer, individual	$12.00
E	Custard, comport	$16.00
	Comport	$75.00
	Dish (Platter), 5"	$8.00
E	Dish (Platter), 6"	$10.00
	Dish (Platter), 7"	$12.00
	Dish (Platter), 9"	$14.00
	Dish (Platter), 10"	$16.00
	Dish (Platter), 11"	$18.00
	Dish (Platter), 12"	$20.00
	Dish (Platter), 14"	$22.00
L	Dish (Platter), 16"	$28.00

	Dish (Platter), 18"	$30.00
	Fruit, 5"	$6.00
	Fruit, 6"	$7.00
	Jug, 36s	$22.00
	Jug, 24s	$36.00
	Jug, 24s	$45.00
	Nappy, 8"	$14.00
	Nappy, 9"	$16.00
	Nappy, 10"	$18.00
	Oatmeal, 36s	$7.00
	Oatmeal, 30s & rim	$6.00
	Pickle	$12.00
	Pickle, fancy	$20.00
	Plate, 5"	$3.00
	Plate, 6"	$5.00
	Plate, 7"	$6.00
	Plate, 8"	$8.00
	Plate, 9"	$9.00
	Plate, 10"	$10.00
	Plate, Coupe, 7"	$8.00
	Plate, Coupe, 8"	$9.00
	Plate, deep Soup	$9.00
E	Plate, Service	$25.00
E	Ramekin	$7.00
E	Ramekin, Saucer	$3.00
	Salad, footed	$18.00
	Sauce Boat	$20.00
	Sauce Boat (Fast Stand)	$24.00
	Sugar	$16.00
	Sugar, individual	$12.00
	Tea Cup	$5.00
	Tea Saucer	$2.50
E	Teapot	$55.00
E	Tureen, sauce (Fast Stand)	$25.00
	Tureen, soup	$55.00

Plate 331: Catalog picture of Edgemore.

1 Bouillon & Saucer
2 Teacup and Saucer
3 Chocolate Cup & Saucer
4 A.D. Coffee & Saucer
5 Butter, individual
6 Fruit
7 Ramekin
8 Ovide Cup & Saucer
9 Coffee Cup & Saucer
10 Sugar
11 Cream
12 Bone Dish

13 Rim Oatmeal
14 Oatmeal
15 Bowl, deep
16 Butter, covered
17 Teapot
18 Sauce Tureen, Fast Stand
19 Sauce Boat, Fast Stand
20 Baker, showing foot
21 Dish, showing foot
22 Nappy
23 Jug
24 Rim Soup

25 Pickle
26 Dish (Platter)
27 Baker
28 Coupe Soup
29 Plate
30 Cake Plate
31 Casserole
32 Soup Tureen
33 Covered Dish
34 Service Plate

Sebring Pottery Company

The Sebring Pottery Company was founded in 1887 in East Liverpool, when the Sebring brothers, George Ashbaugh, and Samson Turnbull took over the Agner Fautts Pottery for $12,500. Ashbaugh and Turnbull sold out their interests soon after the plant was opened. Bill Gates, in his book on the East Liverpool Pottery District, provides interesting details of the events which followed.

In 1893, the Sebrings expanded into East Palestine, Ohio, about 15 miles as the crow flies from East Liverpool. They first leased a plant from the East Palestine Pottery Company, and subsequently built the Ohio China Company, also in East Palestine.

In 1898 the Sebrings gave up the lease in East Palestine and built a pottery in the east end of East Liverpool. This pottery was known as "Klondike" because of its great distance from the center of town. Still, it attracted workers and a small community sprang up around the plant. During the 1890s the plant manufactured plain and decorated semiporcelain and ironstone dinnerware and toilet sets. It also made commemorative plates and specialties. An advertisement in *Crockery and Glass Journal* from 1900 lists an extensive array of these specialties, including ice cream and pudding sets, Egyptian spittoons, and fern dishes, to name but a few.

Requiring larger amounts of room for growth, the Sebring brothers finally decided to resolve the space issue forever, by the simple expedient of purchasing 2000 acres of land in Mahoning County, Ohio, and founding their own town of Sebring. The East Liverpool operations were moved to Sebring, and other potteries were founded there as well. Unlike many of its contemporaries, the Sebring china-making operations survived the Depression, and operated into the 1940s when they were taken over by Anchor Hocking Corporation.

During their Sebring, Ohio, period, the Sebring potteries went through numerous changes in management and name. However, these for the most part take place after the time period that is the focus of this book, so we can safely ignore them until another time.

Plate 332: Sebring backstamp.

**LARGEST PORCELAIN MANUFACTURERS IN THE UNITED STATES.
FOUR PLANTS. 24 WARE KILNS. 24 DECORATING KILNS.
1200 EMPLOYEES. 276,000 SQ. FT. FLOOR SPACE.**

Plate 333: Picture of the Sebring Pottery for 1903 *China, Glass and Lamps* trade magazine.

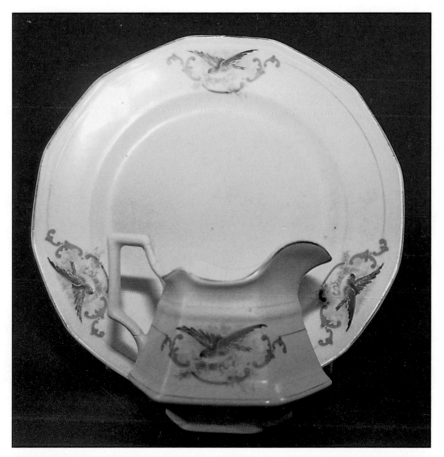

Plate 334: Sebring 100. Unusual shaped 9" plate and creamer of Sebring with the very popular Blue Bird decal. Use value guide page 211.

GLENDORA AND DUTCHESS

The Glendora casserole, shown in Plate 337, is from a small catalog put out by Sebring in 1909. The jumbo coffee, child's set, mustache cup, cake plate, and 30s jug, shown on page 207, Plate 343, are also the Glendora shape. So far only a few pieces of Glendora has been found.

Description of points to look for: The Glendora shape, with its leaf-like embossing (see Plate 336), features flatware that is slightly scalloped with fold-like ridges running down the rim.

The Duchess shape, Plate 337, is also from a small catalog put out by Sebring. To date no pieces of Duchess have been located.

Description of points to look for: Duchess's main feature is a horn-like handle and its scalloped style embossing (see Plate 337). The Duchess flatware may have a scalloped edge similar to that on the casserole lid.

Plate 335: Glendora 100. 13" dish (platter) with pink and yellow daisies and green leaves.

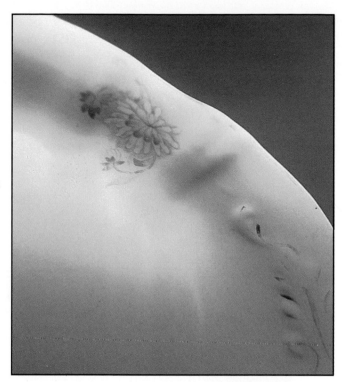

Plate 336: Close-up of embossing found on the Glendora shape.

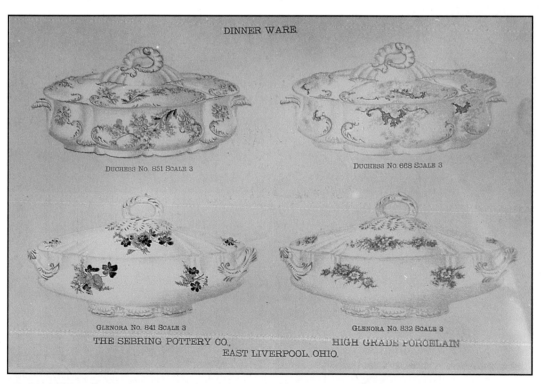

Plate 337: Catalog picture of the Glendora and Duchess shape found at the East Liverpool Museum of Ceramics.

KOKUS

The Kokus shape was shown in *China, Glass, and Lamps* in 1909.

Description of points to look for: A good point of identification could be the finials on the sugar and teapot that are round pointed knobs, but watch out for the ones on the covered dish and butter dish, which are shaped in a plain arch. (This can be seen on the butter in Plate 338.) The flatware is round and oval, with smooth edges with no embossing.

Value guide page 211.

Plate 338: Kokus 100. 7" plate and butter dish.

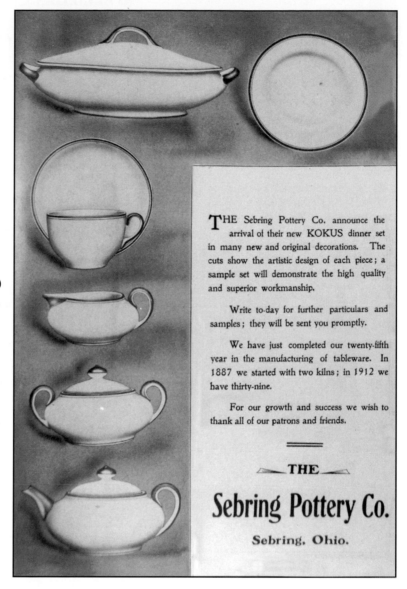

Plate 339: Copy of picture from 1909 *China, Glass, and Lamps* trade magazine.

THE Sebring Pottery Co. announce the arrival of their new KOKUS dinner set in many new and original decorations. The cuts show the artistic design of each piece; a sample set will demonstrate the high quality and superior workmanship.

Write to-day for further particulars and samples; they will be sent you promptly.

We have just completed our twenty-fifth year in the manufacturing of tableware. In 1887 we started with two kilns; in 1912 we have thirty-nine.

For our growth and success we wish to thank all of our patrons and friends.

THE

Sebring Pottery Co.

Sebring, Ohio.

Plate 340: Kokus backstamp from the 7" plate in plate 338.

Plate 341: Kokus backstamp from the butter dish in Plate 337, which Gates and Ormerod date at 1895 and which Gerald DeBolt dates at 1905. These references list this backstamp as having marked ironstone ware, but the butter dish and plate that carries this mark has the feel of semiporcelain.

SPECIALTIES

The next two pages show some of the specialty items made by Sebring.

SPECIALTIES

Jumbo Cup & Saucer ....$35.00 – 45.00	Fancy Plate...........................$18.00 – 28.00
Child's Cup, Saucer & Plate ...$30.00 – 40.00	Jug (small) ....$25.00 – 35.00
Mustache Coffee ....$20.00 – 30.00	Cake Plate ....$15.00 – 25.00
Baby Banana ....$20.00 – 30.00	Fancy Dish...........................$20.00 – 30.00

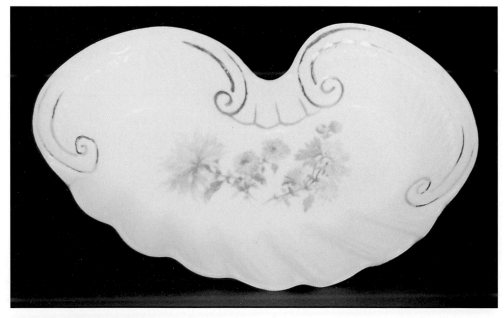

Plate 342: Sebring Banana 100. Baby banana plate pictured in the first row of Plate 343.

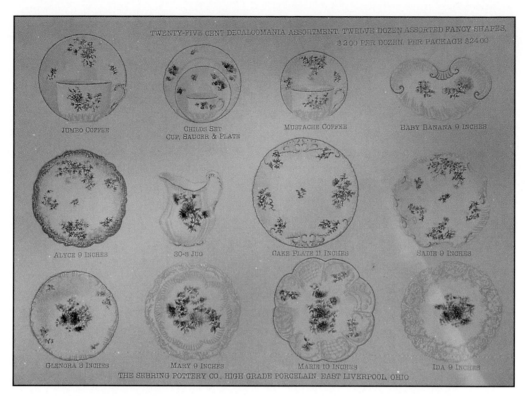

Plate 343: Picture of Sebring specialty items from a catalog at the East Liverpool Museum of Ceramics.

Plate 344: Marie 100. This fancy dish, beautifully embossed, can also be seen in the last row of Plate 343.

SPECIALTIES

Banana Bowl, 12"	$18.00 – 28.00	Bon Bon (3 part)	$15.00 – 20.00
Lemonade Bowl	$60.00 – 70.00	Fern Dish	$25.00 – 35.00
Tuxedo Spittoon	$75.00 – 85.00	Cracker Jar	$20.00 – 30.00
Tokay Dish	$20.00 – 30.00	Ice Cream Tray	$30.00 – 40.00
Orange Bowl	$35.00 – 45.00	Celery Tray	$15.00 – 20.00
Shell Dish	$20.00 – 30.00	Shell Dish	$20.00 – 30.00
Tokay Dish	$20.00 – 30.00	Chocolate Pot	$65.00 – 75.00

Plate 345: Sebring Orange Bowl 100. Orange bowl with brown flower decal.

Plates 346 and **347:** Catalog pictures from the East Liverpool Museum of Ceramics.

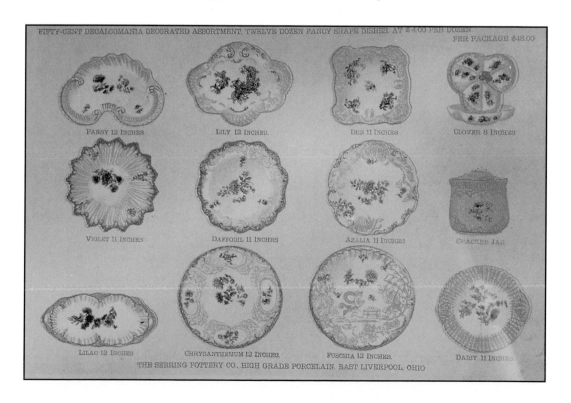

QUEEN

The Queen shape is shown in a 1901 *China, Glass, and Lamps* trade magazine.

Description of points to look for: Queen has a delicate feather-like embossing. (See Plate 348.) Its distinctive finial is an oval with points at three corners and a slightly twisted look. The points on the finial are repeated on the handles but in two spots only. The hollow ware and flatware pieces have scalloped edge. The teapot, sugar, and creamer have paneled straight sides. The covered dish (scc Plate 349) has a pronounced scalloped foot.

Value guide page 211.

Plate 348: Queen 100. Butter dish with insert to drain the butter.

Plate 349: Copy of picture from 1901 *China, Glass, and Lamps* trade magazine.

SEBRING

Baker, 8"................................$14.00 – 18.00	Jug, 3 pt. ....$35.00 – 45.00
Baker, 9"................................$16.00 – 20.00	Jug, 5 pt. ....$40.00 – 55.00
Baker, 10"..............................$18.00 – 24.00	Nappy, 8" ....$14.00 – 18.00
Bone Dish................................$5.00 – 7.00	Nappy, 9" ....$16.00 – 20.00
Bowl, deep, 1 pt....................$10.00 – 14.00	Nappy, 10" ....$18.00 – 24.00
Bowl, deep, 1½ pt. ....$12.00 – 16.00	Oatmeal...................................$6.00 – 8.00
Butter, covered ....$40.00 – 55.00	Pickle ....$14.00 – 24.00
Butter, individual ....$4.50 – 6.00	Plate (Coupe Soup),...............$7.00 – 9.00
Casserole, covered...............$40.00 – 55.00	Plate, 6"...................................$4.50 – 6.00
Coffee Cup ....$8.00 – 10.00	Plate, 7"...................................$5.50 – 7.00
Coffee Saucer ....$5.00 – 7.00	Plate, 8"...................................$7.00 – 8.50
Coffee Saucer, AD ....$5.00 – 7.00	Plate, 9"..................................$8.00 – 10.00
Coffee Cup, AD ....$13.00 – 16.00	Plate, 10"...............................$10.00 – 12.00
Comport ....$55.00 – 75.00	Plate, deep (Rim Soup) ....$8.00 – 10.00
Covered Dish ....$35.00 – 50.00	Sauce Boat ....$18.00 – 22.00
Cream....................................$12.00 – 14.00	Sauce Boat (Fast Stand) ....$22.50 – 25.00
Dish (Platter), 8" ....$10.00 – 12.00	Sauce Boat Stand ....$8.00 – 10.00
Dish (Platter), 9" ....$12.00 – 14.00	Sauce Tureen ....$35.00 – 40.00
Dish (Platter), 11" ....$14.00 – 16.00	Sauce Tureen, Stand ....$10.00 – 12.00
Dish (Platter), 13" ....$16.00 – 18.00	Sauce Tureen, Ladle ....$22.00 – 24.00
Dish (Platter), 15" ....$20.00 – 24.00	Sugar, covered ....$16.00 – 18.00
Dish (Platter), 17" ....$24.00 – 28.00	Teacup (only) ....$5.00 – 7.00
Dish (Platter), 19" ....$26.00 – 32.00	Teacup Saucer (only) ....$2.50 – 4.00
Egg Cup, ...$15.50 – 18.00	Teapot....................................$55.00 – 75.00
Fruit ....$4.00 – 6.00	Tureen, soup ....$55.00 – 80.00
Jug, pt. ....$18.00 – 22.00	Tureen, soup, Ladle ....$24.00 – 26.00
Jug, 1 pt. ....$22.00 – 25.00	

Smith-Phillips China Company

The Smith-Phillips China Company was formed in 1901, taking over a pottery in downtown East Liverpool that was formerly operated by the Sebrings. According to Gates and Ormerod[1], the company initially produced only a single line of dinnerware (called American Girl), plus two toilet ware shapes and a number of specialty items which included cake plates, jugs, nut bowls, and spittoons. *Barber's Book of Marks* refers to American Girl in 1904, when the book was published. In the Wards catalog for 1909 we find Smith-Phillips dinnerware china advertised with the name of "Climbing Rose." This name probably refers to the decoration rather than the shape itself, since the shape is undoubtedly American Girl. The fact that it appears in the Wards catalog is evidence that it was intended for the masses rather than the elite.

By the 1920s Smith-Phillips stopped making of toilet wares and instead added more lines of dinnerware. Advertisements by the company allude to at least two other shapes: Dolly Madison and Princess. The text of one of the advertisements found in the East Liverpool Museum of Ceramics suggests that the Dolly Madison shape preceded Princess. By 1923, the company had confined itself to the production of the Princess shape alone.

In 1929 the company elected to join the ill-fated American Chinaware Corporation, which itself went under two years later, thus following many other illustrious potters into the abyss of the Depression. Wares made by Smith-Phillips are frequently found in antiques shops, rewarding those collectors who have done their homework to memorize the marks of these old potters, and who will take the time to turn over the old-fashioned dishes and examine their backstamps.

A curious footnote to the Smith-Phillips story comes from 1993, when I visited East Liverpool during the Pottery Festival and Collector's Convention. There was a china swap meet held in a building which had "Smith-Phillips" in gold lettering on the display windows. It was clearly an old department store. Why it had the name of the pottery in the windows is not known.

Use the specialty value guide on page 215.

Plate 350: The Smith-Phillips China Company. This picture appears at the top of one of their invoice forms. [From the East Liverpool Museum of Ceramics.]

Plate 351: Smith-Phillips 100. A five-pint jug with large red and yellow roses. The top and bottom look like it was sprayed with several colors of brown.

AMERICAN GIRL

The American Girl shape was produced shortly after the Smith-Phillips China Company was opened in 1901.

Description of points to look for: American Girl hollow ware bodies and lids have a fluted shape. There is also a vine- or scroll-like embossing on both the hollow ware (about the girth of the body and the lid just below the finial) and the flatware. Both the finials and the handles of the hollow ware consist of flattened and embossed circles with a little nub at the outer extremity. The teapot drawing (Plate 356) shows these features. The flatware has an irregular scalloped edge.

Values guide on page 215.

Plate 352: American Girl 100. Casserole and 13" dish (platter) in white and gold.

JUGS

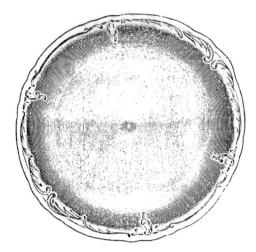

CAKE PLATES

Plate 353, 354, 355, and **356:** American Girl jug, cake plate, bouillon cup and saucer, and teapot from a catalog found at the East Liverpool Ceramics Museum.

BOUILLON CUPS

Plate 357: The American Girl shape from an undated catalog found at the East Liverpool Museum of Ceramics.

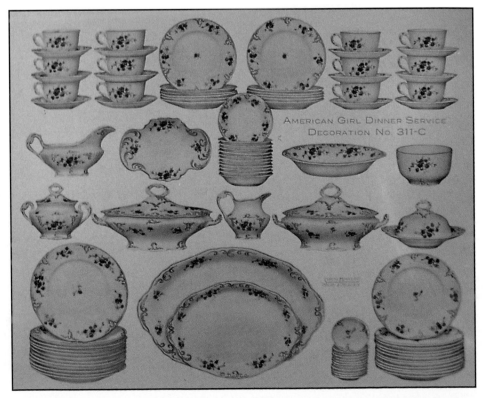

AMERICAN GIRL DINNER SERVICE
DECORATION No. 311-C

AMERICAN GIRL, DOLLY MADISON, and PRINCESS
(D: Dolly Madison only, P: Princess only)

	Baker, 7"	$14.00
D	Baker, 8"	$16.00
	Baker, 9"	$18.50
	Baker, 10"	$22.00
	Bone Dish	$8.00
	Bouillon Cup	$12.00
	Bouillon Saucer	$6.00
	Bowl, deep	$14.00
P	Bowl, oyster	$12.00
	Butter, covered	$55.00
	Butter, individual	$5.00
	Cake Plate, handled	$25.00
D	Casserole, covered, 8"	$40.00
	Casserole, covered, 9"	$45.00
	Casserole, notched cover	$55.00
P	Chocolate Pot	$85.00
P	Chocolate Cup	$10.00
P	Chocolate Saucer	$5.50
P	Chop Plate	$30.00
	Coffee Cup	$10.00
	Coffee Saucer	$6.00
	Coffee, Cup, AD	$14.00
	Coffee Saucer, AD	$6.00
	Covered Dish, 9"	$40.00
	Creamer	$13.50
	Creamer, individual	$11.00
	Cream Soup	$15.00
	Cream Soup Stand	$8.00
	Dish (Platter), 6"	$10.00
	Dish (Platter), 8"	$12.00
	Dish (Platter), 10"	$14.00
	Dish (Platter), 12"	$18.00
	Dish (Platter), 14"	$20.00
	Dish (Platter), 16"	$24.00
P	Egg Cup, sherbet	$18.00
P	Egg Cup, double	$15.00

	Fruit, 4"	$4.50
	Fruit, 5"	$5.00
	Fruit, 6"	$6.00
	Jug, 36s (small)	$20.00
	Jug, 30s (small–medium)	$30.00
	Jug, 24s (medium)	$40.00
	Jug, 12s (large)	$55.00
	Mayonnaise & Stand	$55.00
	Nappy, 8"	$18.00
	Nappy, 9"	$20.00
	Oatmeal, coupe	$7.00
	Oatmeal, rim	$8.00
	Pickle	$16.50
	Plate (Coupe Soup)	$9.00
	Plate, 6"	$5.00
	Plate, 7"	$6.00
	Plate, 8"	$7.50
	Plate, 9"	$9.00
	Plate, 10"	$10.00
	Plate, deep (Rim Soup)	$9.00
P	Ramekin	$9.00
P	Ramekin Plate	$4.50
	Sauce Boat	$18.50
	Sauce Boat (Fast Stand)	$24.00
P	Sauce Ladle	$16.00
P	Sauce Tureen (Fast Stand)	$45.00
P	Sauce Tureen	$35.00
P	Sauce Tureen, Stand	$10.00
P	Soup Ladle	$25.00
	Sugar, covered	$18.00
	Sugar, individual	$14.00
	Teacup (only)	$5.00
	Teacup Saucer (only)	$3.00
	Teapot	$70.00
P	Tureen, oyster	$60.00

DOLLY MADISON

This shape was found mentioned in advertisements in *China, Glass, and Lamps* in 1909. Some pieces have been found both on the West Coast and in the Ohio area. Both the flatware and hollow ware have a fine bead embossing which can be seen on the sauce boat in Plate 360. The finials and handles have elaborate embossing. The flatware has regular scalloped edges. These scallops can also be seen on the pronounced foot of the hollow ware.

Value guide on page 215 .

Plate 358: Dolly Madison 101. Covered dish in white and gold. [From the collection of Bill and Donna Gray.]

Plate 359: Dolly Madison 102. Sugar and creamer from the Thompson House in East Liverpool, Ohio.

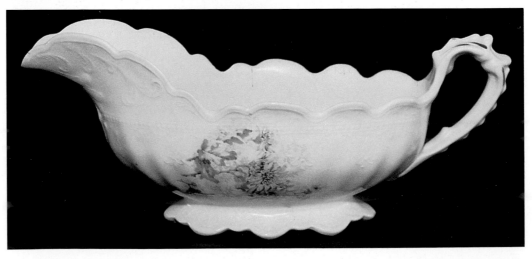

Plate 360: Dolly Madison 100. Sauce boat with violet flowers.

PRINCESS

The Princess shape was advertised in *China, Glass, and Lamps* magazine in many different patterns, one of which was called Cuckoo, which resembled the famous Indian Tree pattern. (See page 250 for information about the Indian Tree pattern.)

Description of points to look for: Princess has no embossing. The flatware consists of smooth rounds and ovals. The best means of identification are the flat topped finials and the graceful looped handles. (See Plate 361.)

Value guide page 215.

Plate 361: Princess 100. Cream and sugar with a band of flowers on a yellow background. There are black and white checkered squares set between the flowers.

Plate 362: Some pieces of the Princess shape. This picture was in the *China, Glass, and Lamps* trade magazine.

Plate 363: Smith-Phillips backstamp found on the creamer and sugar in Plate 361. The date (according to Gerald DeBolt[2]) is 1922.

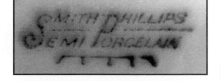

Plate 364: Smith-Phillips backstamp found on the platter shown on American Girl, page 213, Plate 352. Smith-Phillips had an unusual method of dating their china in the early 1900s. According to Gerald DeBolt[2] this date is 1904.

SPECIALTIES

Cake Plate ....$20.00 – 30.00	Orange Bowl............................$35.00 – 45.00
Jumbo Coffee ....$25.00 – 35.00	Plaque (Klondike)...................$18.00 – 28.00
Nut Bowl ....$30.00 – 40.00	Specialty & Advertising Plates .$20.00 – 40.00

Plate 365: This 11" nut bowl has the name of the original owner (Mrs. Ida Honer) inside the bottom in large gold letters.

Plate 366: Two specialty plates. Left: an unidentified scene from antiquity, and right: drafting the Declaration of Independence.

Plate 367: Advertising plate with pheasants.

The history of Vodrey Pottery operation had its beginnings in 1847, when Jabez Vodrey, a native of Staffordshire, England, moved to East Liverpool. Born in 1795, he emigrated to the United States in 1827 and began making pottery in Pittsburgh that same year. He thus became known as "The Father of Potting West of the Alleghenies." Although it was subsequently claimed that this honor belonged to an earlier potter, it cannot be denied that Vodrey was one of the founders of potting in East Liverpool. Vodrey began modestly at first, making clay smoking pipes, then moving on with various partners into the making of Rockingham and yellow ware. Vodrey himself died in 1861, although his company lived on. In 1876 it began the production of ironstone. In 1896 the firm was incorporated as the Vodrey Pottery Company, and added semiporcelain wares to its line. The firm made both white granite and semiporcelain dinnerware sets, toilet wares, and hotel china. The Vodrey Pottery Company ceased operations in 1928, another victim of the terrible financial conditions of the times.

We are fortunate to have obtained catalogs of the wares of the Vodrey Pottery Company from 1913, 1921, and 1926. We find that in 1913 the company offered home dinnerware in the Risco, Bristol, and Melba shapes. At this time, the company also offered hotel wares (heavier, utilitarian ware) and toilet wares in many different shapes. Like other potters of the time, Vodrey also sold both dinnerware and toilet ware in the ubiquitous Cable shape. By 1921, we find that the Risco and Bristol shape has disappeared, although Melba is still offered. Of course, the Hotel, Toilet, and Cable are there as well. In 1926 we find further changes. Melba has been replaced by the Vesta shape, and as before, both Hotel and Cable are available.

Plate 368: Vodrey backstamp.

Plate 369: Specialty plaques in flower designs. They are labeled "Gem Plaques," which suggests they were on the Gem shape. See page 230 for value guide.

Plate 370: A selection of Vodrey specialty plaques adorned with prayers and uplifting moral quotations, probably intended as gifts and presentations.

GEM

Gerald DeBolt[2] dates the Gem mark to 1890 – 1896. He describes this shape as being "a very dense ironstone or semiporcelain." Although the sauce boat in Plate 372 is the only piece of Gem I have found so far, there is sure to be more out there for someone willing to look for it. Watch for the Gem backstamp shown below.

Plate 371: Backstamp found on the Gem sauce boat stand below.

Plate 372: Gem 100. Sauce boat stand in the Gem shape.

The pieces shown below are dated from 1900 or before. The shapes have not been identified. See page 227 for suggested values.

Plate 373: Vodrey 100. This sugar with lid was found in West Virginia. It is covered with a pale blue flowers and brown leaf decoration so popular before the 1900s. Notice heavy slashed embossing on the handles and finial and the finger-like embossing on the base.

Plate 374: Vodrey 101. Sauce boat with unusual flat-topped handle and scalloped foot.

CERAMIC BEAUTY

The Ceramic Beauty shape was introduced on January 1, 1905. This news was published in a trade magazine of that time, together with some examples of what the new shape looked like. Ceramic Beauty has a beaded embossing which can be seen in Plate 375. Another outstanding feature of this shape is its embossed, bow-like finials and casserole handles. The flatware has evenly scalloped edges. The same scalloping is also seen on the hollow ware foot.

For a value guide use the prices on page 227.

Plate 375: Ceramic Beauty 100. 10" plate with delicate green flowers and leaves.

Plate 376: Catalog page showing the Ceramic Beauty shape. This picture is from the files at the East Liverpool Museum of Ceramics.

"The Ceramic Beauty"

Plate 377: An advertisement in a 1904 issue of *China, Glass, and Lamps.*

BRISTOL

The catalog showing this shape was dated 1913. I have not found information which would tell when it was first introduced. Bristol has scalloped embossing. Plate 378 shows this embossing, outlined in gold. It has elaborate, embossed oval finials that have small nubs and equally elaborate handles, also with nubs. Another distinctive feature is the almost ruffed-skirt look on the body of the hollow ware pieces. The flatware has an even scallop on the edge, as does the foot on the casserole, sugar, creamer, and sauce boat.

Value guide page 227.

Plate 378: Bristol 100. 9" plate, sauce boat, sauce boat stand, and sugar with lid. The pattern is of small pink roses and green leaves.

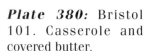

Plate 379: The Bristol shape from a Vodrey catalog found at the East Liverpool Museum of Ceramics.

Plate 380: Bristol 101. Casserole and covered butter.

RISCO

The Risco shape is described in various Vodrey catalogs dating from 1913 to 1921. The Risco shape has light embossing, which becomes heavier around the handles of the flatware serving pieces, as seen at the end of the sauce boat stand in Plate 381. Handles on some pieces of hollow ware come to a point at the top. Most of the finials are smooth and arched (see Plate 382) but note the finial of the covered dish in Plate 383 which looks like an ornate knob. Possibly casseroles and covered dishes were made with both kinds of finials, or there may have been a design change. The flatware has edges with large even scallops.

Value guide page 227.

Plate 381: Risco 100. Sauce boat and sauce boat stand in white and gold.

Plate 382: Risco decorated with pattern #1100.

Plate 383: Risco decorated with pattern #1060¾ from a Vodrey catalog found at the East Liverpool Museum of Ceramics.

MELBA

The Melba shape is shown in the 1913 Vodrey catalog found at the East Liverpool Museum of Ceramics. Melba hollow ware has little or no embossing but the flatware has a delicate flower and leaf-like embossing and is slightly scalloped. Handles and finials are simple loops. What I found most distinctive and interesting was the elongated look of the hollow ware. (See Plate 384.)

Value guide page 227.

Plate 384: Melba 100. Creamer, sugar with lid, and sauce boat in white with gold decoration.

BRISTOL, CERAMIC BEAUTY, MELBA, and RISCO
(M: Melba only, R: Risco only)

Baker, 5"	$12.00
Baker, 8"	$16.00
Baker, 9"	$18.00
Baker, 10"	$20.00
Bone Dish	$8.00
Bouillon	$12.00
Bouillon Saucer	$5.00
Bowl, deep, 1½ pt.	$14.00
Butter, covered	$50.00
Butter, individual	$5.50
Casserole, covered	$40.00
Casserole, notched cover	$50.00
Coffec Cup	$9.00
Coffee Saucer	$6.00
Coffee Saucer, AD	$6.00
Coffee, AD	$14.00
R Covered Dish, 9"	$35.00
Covered Dish, 9½"	$40.00
Cream	$12.00
Dish (Platter), 7"	$12.00
Dish (Platter), 9½"	$14.00
Dish (Platter), 11½"	$18.00
R Dish (Platter), 13"	$20.00
M Dish (Platter), 14"	$22.00
Dish (Platter), 15"	$24.00
Dish (Platter), 17"	$28.00
Egg Cup, unhandled	$15.50
Egg Cup, handled	$18.50
Fruit, 5"	$4.00

Tankard Style:

Jug, 42s (small)	$18.00
Jug, 36s (small–medium)	$25.00
Jug, 30s (medium)	$30.00
Jug, 24s (medium–large)	$40.00
Jug, 12s (large)	$50.00

Low Style:

M	Jug, 24s (medium–large)	$40.00
M	Jug, 12s (large)	$45.00

Covered Jugs:

R	Jug, 42s (small)	$25.00
R	Jug, 36s (small–medium)	$30.00
R	Jug, 30s (medium)	$40.00
R	Jug, 24s (medium–large)	$45.00
R	Jug, 12s (large)	$55.00
	Nappy, 7½"	$16.00
	Nappy, 8"	$18.00
	Nappy, 9½"	$20.00
	Oatmeal, 5½"	$6.00
	Oatmeal, 6½"	$7.00
	Pickle	$20.00
	Plate (Coupe Soup), 7½"	$8.00
	Plate, 6"	$4.50
	Plate, 7"	$5.50
	Plate, 8"	$7.00
	Plate, 9"	$8.00
	Plate, 10"	$9.00
M	Plate, deep (Rim Soup), 8"	$8.00
	Plate, deep (Rim Soup), 9"	$9.00
M	Plaque, 7½"	$22.00
M	Plaque, 8½"	$25.00
M	Plaque, 9½"	$28.00
M	Salad Bowl, embossed	$22.00
M	Salad Bowl, plain	$18.00
R	Salad Plate	$25.00
	Sauce Boat	$18.00
M	Fast Stand, unhandled	$24.50
M	Fast Stand, double handle	$32.00
	Sherbet	$20.00
	Sugar, covered	$18.00
	Teacup (only)	$5.00
	Teacup Saucer (only)	$3.00
	Teapot	$70.00
M	Tea Tile	$35.00

FISH AND GAME SETS

Fish and game sets were very popular around the turn of the century, although they are seen today mostly with foreign marks. The files of the East Liverpool Museum of Ceramics contained these pictures showing the pieces making up their fish and game sets. As seen in Plates 386 and 387, Vodrey sets consisted of a large platter, 12 plates, and a sauce boat. Although a sauce boat would quite naturally go with the service of fish or game, I have never seen a sauce boat included in one of these sets, except for those made by Vodrey.

This is one of the few places where a set would be priced higher than individual pieces.

FISH and GAME SETS			
Dish (Platter)	$55.00 – 75.00	Sauce Boat	$20.00 – 40.00
Plate	$15.00 – 20.00	Set	$275.00 – 375.00

Plate 385: Vodrey 102. This plate with a fish decal was probably part of a fish set similar to the ones seen on the opposite page.

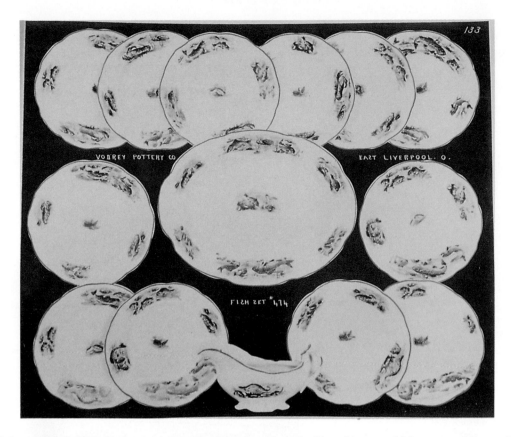

Plates 386 & 387: Vodrey catalog pictures found at the East Liverpool Museum of Ceramics.

SPECIALTIES

There were many catalog pages of beautiful Vodrey speciality plates and plaques. I have picked out just a few to show here.

Plate 388: VodreySpec 103. Specialty plate from the collection of Bill and Donna Gray.

SPECIALTIES	
Plates ....$22.00 – $32.00	
Plaques..............................$30.00 – $40.00	

Plates 389 & 390: Vodrey catalogs of specialty offerings from the East Liverpool Museum of Ceramics.

West End Pottery Company

The West End Pottery Company, located in East Liverpool, Ohio, had a long and colorful history which spanned the peak period of china making in the East Liverpool district. For the historical details of this company, we are especially indebted to Donna Juszczak of the East Liverpool Museum of Ceramics. The story of this company begins with William Burgess and Willis Cunning, who formed a partnership to manufacture potter's supplies in 1885. Three years later, in 1888, they decided to go into the business of making bone china, previously the province of the English pottery industry. Willis Cunning departed for England to study methods for making bone china and to hire men who know how to make it.

Returning to East Liverpool, the two men found the American Bone China Company in 1890. Unfortunately their efforts are not well received in East Liverpool, since the making of bone ash, an essential ingredient for this type of china, creates foul odors. In response to the public outcry, the company took steps to minimize the odors. The company ultimately abandoned the production of bone china for economic reasons. The production was switched instead to the making of white ironstone and semiporcelain china wares under the West End Pottery Company name. In 1893, the company was producing dinnerware, toilet wares, and hotel ware. By the 1920s the company had become one of the most profitable in East Liverpool.

The fortunes of the company began to slip in 1923 with the death of William Burgess, who died while supervising work in the kiln shed. In 1929, West End joined with several other companies to form the American China Corporation. Strangely, in 1930 while still a part of American Chinaware the company began operations under the name of Meric Art Company, which concentrated on the production of fancy wares and art pottery. A year later, in 1931, American Chinaware failed and West End was again on its own. Not surprisingly, in 1933 the company is reported to have begun experiencing financial difficulties.

The final date for the company is uncertain. Lois Lehner[3] reports that the company ceased operation in 1938. However, other sources suggest that operations continued until 1941. It is notable that this date corresponds to the start of World War II. That war had a major impact on the import of chinaware from English and Far Eastern sources. One cannot help but speculate about what might have happened to West End had they been able to participate in the large growth in the domestic china industry during that time.

The company enjoyed a long and productive life, so it is curious that more of their wares are not seen on the antiques market today. Nevertheless, these wares are well worth the effort spent in searching for them, and should be a welcome addition to any collection of old American dinnerware.

Plate 391: Picture of the West End Pottery from the archives of the East Liverpool Museum of Ceramics.

Plate 392: West End 100 (left). Specialty plate with green rim and picture of a lake, trees, and hills. West End 101 (right). Specialty plate with pink rim and castle.

Suggested value of specialty plates see page 245.

DUCHESS

The Duchess shape dates from around 1915. Like other West End pottery, more can be found in the pictures at the East Liverpool Museum of Ceramics than in the antiques stores or flea markets. Duchess has heavy leaf-like embossing that surrounds its finials along with a much more delicate embossing that festoons the rest of its pieces. This can best be seen on the body of the casserole in Plate 393. Its distinctive finial is an oval shape that sweeps into points on each side and one in the middle. The hollow ware has a well-defined scalloped foot, while the flatware has a scalloped edge. Note that the embossing on its jugs is shared with West End's Columbia shape (see page 238, Plate 402).

Value guide page 234.

Plate 393: Duchess 100. Covered dish, white with gold outlining the embossing.

Plate 394: Duchess dinnerware from an old West End catalog in the files of the East Liverpool Museum of Ceramics.

Plate 395: Decoration #3603 on the left and #3618 on the right, on the Duchess shape. From a catalog found at the East Liverpool Museum of Ceramics.

DUCHESS and PURITAN
(D: Dutchess only, P: Puritan only)

P	Baker, 6" $8.50		Dish (Platter), 10".........................$14.00
P	Baker, 7" $12.00		Dish (Platter), 11".........................$16.00
	Baker, 8" $14.00		Dish (Platter), 12".........................$17.00
	Baker, 9" $16.50		Dish (Platter), 13".........................$20.00
	Baker, 10" $18.00		Dish (Platter), 15".........................$24.00
D	Bone Dish $8.00		Dish (Platter), 17".........................$28.00
P	Bowl, deep, 1 pt. $12.00	P	Egg Cup, Footed............................$18.00
	Bowl, deep, 1½ pt. $14.00		Fruit, 5" $5.00
P	Bowl, oyster, 1 pt. $10.00		Fruit, 6" $6.00
P	Bouillon Cup $12.00	P	Grapefruit Bowl, 7" $12.50
P	Bouillon Saucer.........................$4.00	P	Jug, 8 oz. $16.00
	Butter, covered........................$50.00		Jug, 11 oz. $20.00
	Butter, individual.......................$4.00		Jug, 1 pt. $25.00
	Cake Plate, regular $20.00		Jug, 2 pt......................................$38.00
P	Cake Plate, open handle.............$25.00		Jug, 4 pt.......................................$35.00
P	Casserole, covered, 7"...............$30.00		Jug, 5 pt. $40.00
	Casserole, covered, 8"...............$35.00	D	Jug, 7 pt.......................................$50.00
P	Casserole, covered, 9"...............$40.00	P	Nappy, 7".....................................$10.00
P	Casserole, covered, 10".............$45.00		Nappy, 8".....................................$14.00
P	Notched Cover, 7"......................$35.00		Nappy, 9".....................................$16.00
	Notched Cover, 8"......................$40.00		Nappy, 10"...................................$20.00
P	Notched Cover, 9"......................$45.00		Oatmeal, 6"....................................$6.00
P	Notched Cover, 10"....................$50.00	D	Orange Bowl $55.00
D	Celery Tray...............................$25.00		Pickle $15.50
P	Chocolate Cup...........................$10.00		Plate (Coupe Soup), 8"....................$7.00
P	Chocolate Saucer $5.00		Plate, 6" $5.00
	Coffee Cup $8.00		Plate, 7" $6.00
	Coffee Saucer.............................$4.00		Plate, 8" $7.50
	Coffee Saucer, AD $6.00		Plate, 9" $8.00
	Coffee, Cup, AD.........................$12.00		Plate, 10" $10.00
P	Comport, tall footed $75.00		Plate, deep (Rim Soup), 9" $8.00
P	Comport, low unfooted................$45.00		Sauce Boat....................................$18.50
P	Covered Dish, 7"........................$30.00	P	Sauce Boat (Fast Stand) $24.00
	Covered Dish, 8"........................$35.00		Sauce Tureen $35.00
D	Covered Dish, 9"........................$38.00	D	Sauce Tureen Stand........................$10.00
	Covered Dish, 10"......................$40.00		Spoon Tray....................................$40.00
	Covered Dish, 11"......................$42.00		Sugar, covered $18.00
P	Creamer, 8 oz............................$10.50		Sugar, individual $13.00
P	Creamer, 11 oz...........................$12.50		Teacup (only) $5.00
	Creamer, 1 pt. $14.00		Teacup Saucer (only)......................$3.00
P	Custard, footed..........................$14.00		Teapot $65.00
P	Dish (Platter), 9"........................$8.00	P	Tureen, oyster $60.00

Plate 396: Catalog picture of Dutchess.

Plate 397: Catalog picture of Puritan.

PURITAN

The Puritan shape, which generally dates from the first or second decade of the twentieth century, presents a simple, unadorned appearance, devoid of embossing. The flatware is undistinguished. Hollow ware may be identified by the general outline of its smooth, sloping sides. The handles are easy-to-grasp loops. The finials, its most distinctive feature, are rectangular with a depressed center. This attractive shape was a perfect background for the bright designs used to decorate it. It is unfortunate that it has proven so difficult to locate.

Value guide page 234.

Plate 398: Puritan 100. This 10" plate shows some to the beautiful patterns that were shown on this shape. This may have been West End's version of the famous Indian Tree pattern.

Plates 399 & 400: Puritan dinnerware from an West End catalog at the East Liverpool Museum of Ceramics.

Plate 401: A selection of patterns on the Puritan shape from a catalog at the East Liverpool Museum of Ceramics.

COLUMBIA

The Columbia shape dates from around 1915. Columbia has rather unusual embossing. As seen on the small jug shown below, the fan-shaped embossing is set very deeply into the roundest part of the piece. Finials and handles are elaborate, with nubs at different points. Flatware has scalloped embossing. This shape is rare and difficult to locate.

Value guide page 241.

Plate 402: Columbia 100. Small jug with mulberry-colored flowers.

Plate 403: Backstamp of the jug shown above.

Plate 404: Columbia dinnerware from a catalog at the East Liverpool Museum of Ceramics.

SENECA

This shape (not to be confused with HLC's Seneca shape) dates from the 1920s and is thicker in appearance and heavier in weight than other pieces of West End china I have found. It has almost the feel of hotel china, but there was no indication that this was other than regular dinnerware. Seneca has no embossing. It has a very plain, arch-style finial. The flatware has smooth edges and occurs in both round and oval shapes.

Value guide page 241.

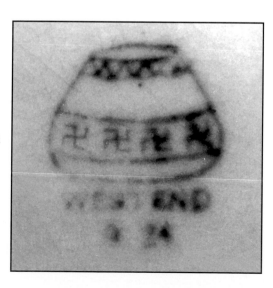

Plate 405: Backstamp of the pickle dish shown in Plate 407.

Plate 406: Pattern #S-38520-A, a representative piece of Seneca dinnerware from a catalog at the East Liverpool Museum of Ceramics.

Plate 407: Seneca 100. Pickle dish with fancy band style decoration.

SENECA and COLUMBIA
(S: Seneca only, C: Columbia only)

	Baker, 6"	$8.50	S	Egg Cup, footed	$18.00
	Baker, 7"	$12.00		Fruit, 5"	$5.00
	Baker, 8"	$14.00		Fruit, 6"	$6.00
S	Baker, 9"	$16.50	S	Grapefruit Bowl, 7"	$12.50
S	Baker, 10"	$18.00		Jug, 11 oz.	$20.00
C	Bone Dish	$6.00		Jug, 1 pt.	$25.00
S	Bowl, deep, 1 pt.	$12.00		Jug, 2 pt.	$38.00
	Bowl, deep, 1½ pt.	$14.00		Jug, 4 pt.	$35.00
	Bowl, oyster, 1 pt.	$10.00		Jug, 5 pt.	$40.00
	Butter, covered	$55.00		Jug, 7 pt.	$50.00
	Butter, individual	$4.00		Nappy, 7"	$10.00
	Cake Plate, regular	$20.00		Nappy, 8"	$14.00
	Cake Plate, open handle	$25.00		Nappy, 9"	$16.00
	Casserole, covered, 8"	$30.00		Nappy, 10"	$20.00
	Casserole, covered, 9"	$35.00		Nappy, 11"	$25.00
S	Notched Cover, 8"	$40.00		Oatmeal, 6"	$6.00
	Notched Cover, 9"	$45.00		Pickle	$15.50
C	Chop Plate	$25.00		Plate (Coupe Soup), 8"	$7.00
	Coffee Cup	$6.00		Plate, 6"	$5.00
	Coffee Saucer	$4.00		Plate, 7"	$6.00
S	Coffee Saucer, AD	$6.00		Plate, 8"	$7.50
S	Coffee, Cup, AD	$14.00		Plate, 9"	$8.00
	Comport, tall footed	$75.00		Plate, 10"	$10.00
	Comport, low unfooted	$45.00		Plate, deep (Rim Soup), 9"	$8.00
	Covered Dish, 10"	$38.00		Sauce Boat	$18.50
S	Covered Dish, 11"	$42.00		Sauce Boat (Fast Stand)	$24.00
	Creamer	$12.00		Sugar, covered	$18.00
S	Custard, footed	$14.00		Sugar, individual	$13.00
C	Dish (Platter), 7"	$8.00		Teacup (only)	$5.00
	Dish (Platter), 10"	$14.00		Teacup Saucer (only)	$3.00
	Dish (Platter), 11"	$16.00		Teapot	$65.00
S	Dish (Platter), 12"	$17.00		Tureen, oyster	$60.00
	Dish (Platter), 14"	$20.00		Tureen, Stand	$15.00
	Dish (Platter), 16"	$24.00		Tureen, Ladle	$25.00
	Dish (Platter), 18"	$28.00			

Plate 408: Catalog picture of Seneca.

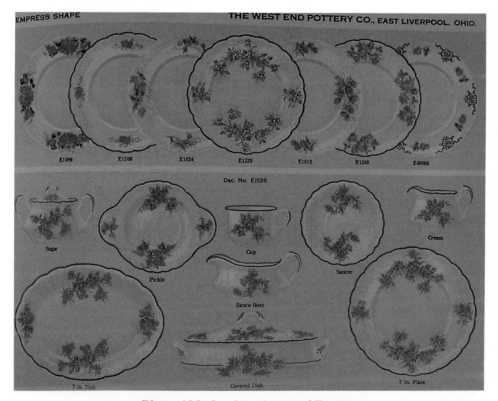

Plate 409: Catalog picture of Empress.

This unidentified shape dates from the 1920s or 1930s. It has been found both in California and Ohio. Every piece discovered so far has been beautifully decorated. It is unfortunate than its name remains a mystery. Most pieces of this shape have no embossing. The creamer has a smooth rounded handle, while the sugar has a button-like finial and an unusual, wide rim around the lid which has handles embossed into it. (See Plate 412.) I bid on the matching casserole (which looks just like the sugar, but larger) at the annual antique china auction in Wellsville, Ohio, but another collector wanted it much worse than I. The flatware has smooth edges and comes in both round and oval shapes. Of special note is the embossed handle on butter/muffin plate in Plate 411.

Value guide page 241.

Plate 410: Backstamp of the platter shown below.

Plate 411: West End 100. 15" platter, saucer for butter dish or muffin, and 7" plate with a band of pink and blue flowers and yellow leaves on a black background.

Plate 412: West End 101. Cream and sugar with very colorful pink roses.

SPECIALTIES

Here are just a few of the many specialties made by the West End China Company. The following catalog pages, which came from the East Liverpool Museum of Ceramics, are all beautifully handtinted. This was a frequent practice among the old pottery firms, before the days of color photography and printing, when they needed to show off their decorations.

Plate 413: West End Spec 100. Seven-piece fish set. West End also made game and turkey sets.

SPECIALTIES

Fish, Game, or Turkey Sets..$145.00 – 200.00
Specialty or Advertising Plates...$20.00 – 30.00
Plaques ....$25.00 – 50.00
Salad Bowls...$20.00 – 30.00
Cake Plates ....$20.00 – 25.00

Plate 414: West End Spec 101. Beautiful hand-painted plaques.

Plate 415: Yale pattern fancy salad bowls. These are in the first three rows. Harvard pattern fancy salad bowls are in the last two rows.

Value Guide Information

Placing a value on antique china is somewhat of a subjective process, and the values shown on the pages in this book are to be taken as a guide only. The values given are for pieces in pristine condition. The values are affected by the following factors:

Decoration — Pieces which are decorated in an interesting and pleasing manner are worth more than those whose decorations are common and uninspired.

Workmanship — Pieces which are shaped as the manufacturer intended are worth more than those which are warped or otherwise misshapen. Similarly, decorations which are applied evenly and with skill will increase the value of a piece, while those which are uneven or out of place will reduce its value.

Demand — In the last reckoning, value is established by the laws of supply and demand. These rules will prevail in cases where certain decorations (such as the blue bird patterns) or individual pieces are specifically and avidly collected by groups of people. Spoon holders (spooners) and teapots are examples of pieces subject to this type of upward pressure on value.

Wear and Damage — A missing lid of a piece which was originally accompanied by a lid will reduce its value by half. A chip in a visible place will also reduce the value by a similar factor. Cracks will reduce value, the amount in proportion to the extent of the crack and its visibility. Finally, value is reduced by wear which affects the decoration. Gold and platinum are particularly subject to wear, since they are unprotected by any glazing.

In the pages which follow, suggested values are provided for each of the shapes described in this book. For each of the shapes, a complete list of all of the pieces that a specific pottery identified as making up that shape are shown whenever possible. A generic list is used where no list was available. In each of these lists, the trade names (rather than common names) are used. To translate trade names to common names, refer to the section on Naming and Sizing of Antique China Pieces.

Naming and Sizing of Antique China Pieces

The methods used to identify and size pieces of china are rooted in the history of the trade, and were certainly not chosen with the interests of the antiques collector in mind. Unfortunately, it is sometimes impossible to avoid these arcane measurement systems, since often the only clue as to what a particular piece is will be found in an old trade catalog which uses these quaint terms. I found the process of learning about these old methods to be quite fascinating. Those of you who have been truly bitten with the old china bug will, I'm sure, find the information below to be most helpful.

Size of Pieces

The different systems that are known to have been used at various times to size old china include any of the following, used separately or in combination with one another:

- The number of pieces that will fit in a barrel, the normal shipment method in earlier times. A reference of 30s or 36s typically will designate how many of that piece will fit into a barrel. Note that the larger the number, the smaller the size of an individual piece, and hence the greater quantity that will fit into the barrel.

- Capacity, in ounces or pints. This measurement, of course, only applied to hollow ware. This information can be particularly useful when one is attempting to determine whether a creamer is the standard variety or an individual creamer. Volumetric measurement appears to be used only with pieces intended to contain fluids.

- Linear measurement, in inches. The size, however, is usually a trade size, and not always the actual size that you will measure with your ruler. Thus a 9" baker may have an actual length of 9⅛ inches.

Having dealt with the matter of sizing, one must address the trade names of the various shapes. These names, for the most part, are inherited from the English china-making tradition. Names such as "nappy" and "baker" are certain to catch one's attention. However, the collector must also be aware that a "dish" is in reality a platter. On the following pages I have listed some of the trade names that will be encountered in the value guide together with today's common name for the piece, as well as other interesting information.

NAME	INFORMATION
A.D. Cup	Small size cup for after-dinner coffee.
Baker	Oval, uncovered vegetable bowl.
Baltimore	A style of cup and saucer used by many potteries and added to many different sets, from hotel ware to some very fancy sets.
Bon Bon	Dish used for candy.
Bone Dish	Chicken or fish bones were placed in this special dish which was placed close beside the upper right of the plate.
Boston	A style of cup and saucer used by many potteries and added to many different sets, from hotel ware to some very fancy sets.
Bouillon Cup	Shaped like a teacup with two handles.
Boule	A style of cup and saucer used by many potteries and added to many different sets, from hotel ware to some very fancy sets.
Casserole	Round, covered vegetable bowl.
Chop Plate	A large round or square serving platter, 12 to 20 inches in diameter.
Coffee Cup	Oversized cup generally used for serving breakfast coffee.
Comport	A fruit or candy dish raised upon a stem.
Compote	Same as comport.
Comportier	Same as comport (sometimes of fancy design).
Coupe Soup	Shallow, flat bowl generally 7 or 8 inches in diameter.
Covered Dish	Same as a casserole but oblong instead of round.
Cracker Jar	Also called a biscuit jar, used for crackers and biscuits.
Cream Soup	Two-handled soup used with a saucer underneath for an informal table.
Custard	Dessert cup on a stem with or without a handle.
Deep Bowl	Round deep container.
Demi-tasse (AD)	Small, after-dinner china pieces. Usually cup and saucer, coffee pot, creamer, and sugar.
Dish	Platter.
Fruit	Sauce or dessert dish.
Jug	Pitcher.

Nappy	Round, uncovered vegetable bowl.
Newport	Square, uncovered serving bowl.
Onion or Lug Soup	Handles are tabs instead of pierced loops. Contents slightly more than a cream soup, about the size of an oatmeal.
Oatmeal	Much the same as a fruit but larger, usually around 6" and used for cereal.
Ovide	A style of cup and saucer used by many potteries and added to many different sets, from hotel ware to some very fancy sets.
Oyster Bowl	Similar to a deep bowl but usually very plain and heavy with a pronounced foot.
Pickle	A small oval platter measuring about 9 inches.
Plate 6"	Bread and butter plate.
Plate 7"	Dessert plate.
Plate 8"	Breakfast or salad plate.
Plate 9"	Luncheon or small dinner plate.
Plate 10"	Large dinner plate.
Plate, Deep	Rimmed soup, same as a coupe soup but with a rim or shoulder and used on a formal table.
Ramekin	Small dish with flat, extended rims, sometimes accompanied by a plate. Used for individual portions.
Rim Soup	Shallow soup bowl with rim or shoulder.
St. Denis	A style of cup and saucer used by many potteries and added to many different sets, from hotel ware to some very fancy sets.
Sauce Boat, Fast Stand	Gravy boat with attached underplate.
Saxon	A style of cup and saucer used by many potteries and added to many different sets, from hotel ware to some very fancy sets.
Service Plate	Large under-plate usually ornately decorated.
Teacup	Conventional size used in America for tea or coffee.
Tureen	A deep vessel (often oval) with a lid, notched for a ladle, from which soup is served. Also a smaller vessel of similar shape for sauce or gravy.
Waldorf	A style of cup and saucer used by many potteries and added to many different sets, from hotel ware to some very fancy sets.

Glossary

Bisque	China pieces which have received their first firing, but have not yet been glazed. Bisque is generally rather porous and thus is not suitable for use until after it has received a glaze.
C.C. Ware	An abbreviation for cream colored ware. Ware usually has a hard alkaline glaze. It was made by many potteries in the United States from 1850 to 1900.
Decal or Decalcomania	The slide-off decalcomania is a combination of two processes. The pattern is silk screened or lithographed onto a gelatin sur face backed by a heavy paper. This forms a decalcomania which is then transferred to the ware by soaking the paper so that the gelatin softens and slides off. Excess water and air are squeezed out with a squeegee, and the piece is ready for firing. The gelatin burns out in the kiln, leaving the colored pattern on the ware.
Embossed	A raised design formed from the clay body of a dish, as opposed to being applied to the body afterwards.
Finial	A handle on top of a lid.
Flatware	Plates, platter, and the like. Generally, any flat dish.
Foot	An extension of the bottom of a dish upon which the dish rests.
Glaze	The glossy, glass-like coating that is applied over the surface of ware and melted in the ovens to a smooth surface. This covering makes the ware impermeable to fluids, protects any decoration under the glaze, and provides a decorative luster. It may be clear, opaque, or colored. Glaze is usually applied by spraying, painting, or dipping.
Hand painted	It may be the entire pattern or merely lines and touching up. Sometimes outlines are printed on the ware and patterns filled in by hand.
Hollow ware	Dishes with raised sides and sometimes with covers, generally intended to contain liquids or similar substances. Bowls, creamers, sugar bowls, casseroles, cups, teapots, etc.
Indian Tree	The Indian Tree pattern goes back to around 1780. Its picture, which has an Oriental look, usually covers the well of a plate and consists of a nearly bare, crooked tree which shoots upward. The

tree and its off-shooting branches, as well as other parts of the china, are covered with leaves and flowers. There is sometimes a bird on one of the branches. Each pottery has its own variation of this theme.

Ironstone	This is a process for making a dense, hard-bodied ware with a pure white body and a clear hard glaze.
Matte	A dull, non-reflective glaze or other surface finish.
Moss Rose	Pattern of roses and their foliage popular during the 1880s and 1890s. While different potters may have had their variation of this pattern it usually consisted of four large pink rosebuds with long stems which are gathered together, the center of the stems are large rose leaves.
Overglaze	Decorations are applied after the glaze has been fired since certain colors fade under the intense heat used in firing the glaze.
Rim	The raised outer portion of a dish, usually of a plate or bowl.
Semiporcelain	Ware that is vitreous. Because it is not translucent it is not porcelain. It was used for decorated tableware and was lighter and more graceful than white granite. It first made its appearance in the United States in the later part of the 1800s.
Stamped	Designs applied by hand with rubber stamps.
Transfer Printing	A design is cut into copper or steel plates. A color is washed over the plates. The design is then transferred from the plates to a thin paper. The paper is then used to transfer the design to the piece of ware.
Underglaze	Decorations are applied directly to the ware and then coated over with a glaze. Decoration applied in this way cannot wear off unless the glaze itself is broken.
Verge	The point at which the sides of the dish turn upward from the well.
Well	The generally flat bottom of a dish.
White Granite	White ware with great hardness and density made by many American potters between 1860 and 1900. Also known as ironstone, stoneware, and other various names.
White Ware	General name that covers anything from white earthenware to stoneware to semiporcelain.

Endnotes

1. Gates, W. and D, Ormerod. *The East Liverpool, Ohio, Pottery District.* The Society for Historical Anthropology, 1982.

2. DeBolt, Gerald. *Dictionary of American Pottery Marks.* Paducah, KY: Collector Books, 1994.

3. Lehner, Lois. *Lehner's Encyclopedia of U.S. Marks on Pottery, Porcelain, & Clay.* Paducah, KY: Collector Books, 1988.

4. Kamm, Minnie Watson. *Old China.* Published privately by Mrs. Kamm in 1951. The book contains the note: "Copies of this book may be obtained from Mrs. Oliver Kamm, 365 Lake Shore Road, Grosse Pointe Farms 30, Michigan. Price: Two Dollars and Twenty Five Cents." I have not tried to obtain a copy from this address, and it is doubtful if one could 44 years after the note was published. I obtained a copy for $50.00 from a private party, who I contacted through an advertisement I published for that purpose. This book contains a wealth of information about the very earliest American dinnerware shapes.

5. Ayers, Walter. *Larkin China.* Summerdale, PA: Echo Publishing, 1990. This book is a collection of advertisements put out over the years by the Larkin Soap Company, who offered china (by HLC and others) as premiums for the purchase of their soap products.

COLLECTOR BOOKS

Informing Today's Collector

For over two decades we have been keeping collectors informed on trends and values in all fields of antiques and collectibles.

DOLLS, FIGURES & TEDDY BEARS

2382	**Advertising Dolls**, Identification & Values, Robison & Sellers	$9.95
2079	**Barbie** Doll Fashions, Volume I, Eames	$24.95
3957	**Barbie** Exclusives, Rana	$18.95
4557	**Barbie**, The First 30 Years, Deutsch	$24.95
3310	**Black Dolls**, 1820–1991, Perkins	$17.95
3873	**Black Dolls**, Book II, Perkins	$17.95
3810	**Chatty Cathy** Dolls, Lewis	$15.95
2021	Collectible **Action Figures**, 2nd Ed., Manos	$14.95
1529	Collector's Encyclopedia of **Barbie** Dolls, DeWein	$19.95
4506	Collector's Guide to **Dolls in Uniform**, Bourgeois	$18.95
3727	Collector's Guide to **Ideal Dolls**, Izen	$18.95
3728	Collector's Guide to Miniature **Teddy Bears**, Powell	$17.95
3967	Collector's Guide to **Trolls**, Peterson	$19.95
4569	**Howdy Doody**, Collector's Reference and Trivia Guide, Koch	$16.95
1067	**Madame Alexander** Dolls, Smith	$19.95
3971	**Madame Alexander** Dolls Price Guide #20, Smith	$9.95
3733	**Modern Collector's** Dolls, Sixth Series, Smith	$24.95
3991	**Modern Collector's** Dolls, Seventh Series, Smith	$24.95
4571	**Liddle Kiddles**, Identification & Value Guide, Langford	$18.95
3972	Patricia Smith's **Doll Values**, Antique to Modern, 11th Edition	$12.95
3826	Story of **Barbie**, Westenhouser	$19.95
1513	**Teddy Bears & Steiff** Animals, Mandel	$9.95
1817	**Teddy Bears & Steiff** Animals, 2nd Series, Mandel	$19.95
2084	**Teddy Bears, Annalee's & Steiff** Animals, 3rd Series, Mandel	$19.95
1808	Wonder of **Barbie**, Manos	$9.95
1430	World of **Barbie** Dolls, Manos	$9.95

FURNITURE

1457	American **Oak** Furniture, McNerney	$9.95
3716	American **Oak** Furniture, Book II, McNerney	$12.95
1118	Antique **Oak** Furniture, Hill	$7.95
2132	Collector's Encyclopedia of **American** Furniture, Vol. I, Swedberg	$24.95
2271	Collector's Encyclopedia of **American** Furniture, Vol. II, Swedberg	$24.95
3720	Collector's Encyclopedia of **American** Furniture, Vol. III, Swedberg	$24.95
1437	Collector's Guide to **Country** Furniture, Raycraft	$9.95
3878	Collector's Guide to **Oak** Furniture, George	$12.95
1755	Furniture of the **Depression Era**, Swedberg	$19.95
3906	**Heywood-Wakefield** Modern Furniture, Rouland	$18.95
1965	**Pine** Furniture, Our American Heritage, McNerney	$14.95
1885	**Victorian** Furniture, Our American Heritage, McNerney	$9.95
3829	**Victorian** Furniture, Our American Heritage, Book II, McNerney	$9.95
3869	**Victorian** Furniture books, 2 volume set, McNerney	$19.90

JEWELRY, HATPINS, WATCHES & PURSES

1712	Antique & Collector's **Thimbles** & Accessories, Mathis	$19.95
1748	Antique **Purses**, Revised Second Ed., Holiner	$19.95
1278	Art Nouveau & Art Deco **Jewelry**, Baker	$9.95
4558	Christmas Pins, Past and Present, Gallina	$18.95
3875	Collecting Antique **Stickpins**, Kerins	$16.95
3722	Collector's Ency. of **Compacts, Carryalls & Face Powder Boxes**, Mueller	$24.95
3992	Complete Price Guide to **Watches**, #15, Shugart	$21.95
1716	Fifty Years of Collectible **Fashion Jewelry**, 1925-1975, Baker	$19.95
1424	**Hatpins** & Hatpin Holders, Baker	$9.95
4570	Ladies' **Compacts**, Gerson	$24.95
1181	100 Years of Collectible **Jewelry**, 1850-1950, Baker	$9.95
2348	20th Century Fashionable Plastic **Jewelry**, Baker	$19.95
3830	Vintage **Vanity Bags & Purses**, Gerson	$24.95

TOYS, MARBLES & CHRISTMAS COLLECTIBLES

3427	**Advertising Character** Collectibles, Dotz	$17.95
2333	Antique & Collector's **Marbles**, 3rd Ed., Grist	$9.95
3827	Antique & Collector's **Toys**, 1870–1950, Longest	$24.95
3956	Baby Boomer **Games**, Identification & Value Guide, Polizzi	$24.95
3717	**Christmas** Collectibles, 2nd Edition, Whitmyer	$24.95
1752	**Christmas** Ornaments, Lights & Decorations, Johnson	$19.95
3874	Collectible Coca-Cola Toy **Trucks**, deCourtivron	$24.95
2338	Collector's Encyclopedia of **Disneyana**, Longest, Stern	$24.95
2151	Collector's Guide to **Tootsietoys**, 2nd Ed., Richter	$16.95
3436	Grist's Big Book of **Marbles**	$19.95
3970	Grist's Machine-Made & Contemporary **Marbles**, 2nd Ed.	$9.95
3732	**Matchbox®** Toys, 1948 to 1993, Johnson	$18.95
3823	**Mego** Toys, An Illustrated Value Guide, Chrouch	15.95
1540	**Modern Toys** 1930–1980, Baker	$19.95
3888	**Motorcycle** Toys, Antique & Contemporary, Gentry/Downs	$18.95
3891	Schroeder's Collectible **Toys**, Antique to Modern Price Guide, 2nd Ed.	$17.95
1886	Stern's Guide to **Disney** Collectibles	$14.95
2139	Stern's Guide to **Disney** Collectibles, 2nd Series	$14.95
3975	Stern's Guide to **Disney** Collectibles, 3rd Series	$18.95
2028	**Toys**, Antique & Collectible, Longest	$14.95
3975	**Zany Characters** of the Ad World, Lamphier	$16.95

INDIANS, GUNS, KNIVES, TOOLS, PRIMITIVES

1868	Antique **Tools**, Our American Heritage, McNerney	$9.95
2015	Archaic **Indian** Points & Knives, Edler	$14.95
1426	**Arrowheads** & Projectile Points, Hothem	$7.95
2279	**Indian** Artifacts of the Midwest, Hothem	$14.95
3885	**Indian** Artifacts of the Midwest, Book II, Hothem	$16.95
1964	**Indian** Axes & Related Stone Artifacts, Hothem	$14.95
2023	**Keen Kutter** Collectibles, Heuring	$14.95
3887	Modern **Guns**, Identification & Values, 10th Ed., Quertermous	$12.95
4505	Standard Guide to **Razors**, Ritchie & Stewart	$9.95
3325	Standard **Knife** Collector's Guide, 2nd Ed., Ritchie & Stewart	$12.95

PAPER COLLECTIBLES & BOOKS

1441	Collector's Guide to **Post Cards**, Wood	$9.95
2081	Guide to Collecting **Cookbooks**, Allen	$14.95
3969	Huxford's **Old Book** Value Guide, 7th Ed.	$19.95
3821	Huxford's **Paperback** Value Guide	$19.95
2080	Price Guide to **Cookbooks & Recipe Leaflets**, Dickinson	$9.95
2346	**Sheet Music** Reference & Price Guide, 2nd Ed., Pafik & Guiheen	$18.95

GLASSWARE

1006	**Cambridge Glass** Reprint 1930–1934	$14.95
1007	**Cambridge Glass** Reprint 1949–1953	$14.95
2310	**Children's Glass Dishes, China & Furniture**, Vol. I, Lechler	$19.95
1627	**Children's Glass Dishes, China & Furniture**, Vol. II, Lechler	$19.95
4561	Collectible **Drinking Glasses**, Chase & Kelly	$17.95
3719	Coll. **Glassware** from the 40's, 50's & 60's, 3rd Ed., Florence	$19.95
2352	Collector's Encyclopedia of **Akro Agate** Glassware, Florence	$14.95
1810	Collector's Encyclopedia of **American Art Glass**, Shuman	$29.95
3312	Collector's Encyclopedia of **Children's Dishes**, Whitmyer	$19.95
3724	Collector's Encyclopedia of **Depression Glass**, 12th Ed., Florence	$19.95
1664	Collector's Encyclopedia of **Heisey Glass**, 1925–1938, Bredehoft	$24.95
3905	Collector's Encyclopedia of **Milk Glass**, Newbound	$24.95
1523	Colors In **Cambridge Glass**, National Cambridge Soceity	$19.95

COLLECTOR BOOKS
Informing Today's Collector

4564	**Crackle Glass**, Weitman	$18.95
2275	**Czechoslovakian Glass** and Collectibles, Barta	$16.95
3882	**Elegant Glassware** of the Depression Era, 6th Ed., Florence	$19.95
1380	Encyclopedia of **Pattern Glass**, McClain	$12.95
3981	Ever's Standard **Cut Glass** Value Guide	$12.95
3725	**Fostoria**, Pressed, Blown & Hand Molded Shapes, Kerr	$24.95
3883	**Fostoria Stemware**, The Crystal for America, Long & Seate	$24.95
3318	**Glass Animals** of the Depression Era, Garmon & Spencer	$19.95
3886	**Kitchen Glassware** of the Depression Years, 5th Ed., Florence	$19.95
2394	**Oil Lamps II**, Glass Kerosene Lamps, Thuro	$24.95
3889	Pocket Guide to **Depression Glass**, 9th Ed., Florence	$9.95
3739	Standard Encyplopedia of **Carnival Glass**, 4th Ed., Edwards	$24.95
3740	Standard **Carnival Glass** Price Guide, 9th Ed.	$9.95
3974	Standard Encyplopedia of **Opalescent Glass**, Edwards	$19.95
1848	**Very Rare Glassware** of the Depression Years, Florence	$24.95
2140	**Very Rare Glassware** of the Depression Years, 2nd Series, Florence	$24.95
3326	**Very Rare Glassware** of the Depression Years, 3rd Series, Florence	$24.95
3909	**Very Rare Glassware** of the Depression Years, 4th Series, Florence	$24.95
2224	World of **Salt Shakers**, 2nd Ed., Lechner	$24.95

3314	Collector's Encyclopedia of **Van Briggle** Art Pottery, Sasicki	$24.95
2111	Collector's Encyclopedia of **Weller Pottery**, Huxford	$29.95
3452	Coll. Guide to Country Stoneware & Pottery, Raycraft	$11.95
2077	Coll. Guide to **Country Stoneware & Pottery**, 2nd Series, Raycraft	$14.95
3433	Collector's Guide To **Harker Pottery** - U.S.A., Colbert	$17.95
3434	Coll. Guide to **Hull Pottery**, The Dinnerware Line, Gick-Burke	$16.95
3876	Collector's Guide to **Lu-Ray Pastels**, Meehan	$18.95
3814	Collector's Guide to **Made in Japan** Ceramics, White	$18.95
4565	Collector's Guide to **Rockingham**, The Enduring Ware, Brewer	$14.95
2339	Collector's Guide to **Shawnee Pottery**, Vanderbilt	$19.95
1425	**Cookie Jars**, Westfall	$9.95
3440	**Cookie Jars**, Book II, Westfall	$19.95
3435	Debolt's Dictionary of **American Pottery Marks**	$17.95
2379	Lehner's Ency. of **U.S. Marks** on Pottery, Porcelain & China	$24.95
3825	**Puritan Pottery**, Morris	$24.95
1670	**Red Wing Collectibles**, DePasquale	$9.95
1440	**Red Wing Stoneware**, DePasquale	$9.95
3738	**Shawnee Pottery**, Mangus	$24.95
3327	**Watt Pottery** – Identification & Value Guide, Morris	$19.95

POTTERY

1312	**Blue & White Stoneware**, McNerney	$9.95
1958	So. Potteries **Blue Ridge Dinnerware**, 3rd Ed., Newbound	$14.95
1959	**Blue Willow**, 2nd Ed., Gaston	$14.95
3816	Collectible **Vernon Kilns**, Nelson	$24.95
3311	Collecting **Yellow Ware** – Id. & Value Guide, McAllister	$16.95
1373	Collector's Encyclopedia of **American Dinnerware**, Cunningham	$24.95
3815	Collector's Encyclopedia of **Blue Ridge Dinnerware**, Newbound	$19.95
2272	Collector's Encyclopedia of **California Pottery**, Chipman	$24.95
3811	Collector's Encyclopedia of **Colorado Pottery**, Carlton	$24.95
2133	Collector's Encyclopedia of **Cookie Jars**, Roerig	$24.95
3723	Collector's Encyclopedia of **Cookie Jars**, Volume II, Roerig	$24.95
3429	Collector's Encyclopedia of **Cowan Pottery**, Saloff	$24.95
2209	Collector's Encyclopedia of **Fiesta**, 7th Ed., Huxford	$19.95
3961	Collector's Encyclopedia of **Early Noritake**, Alden	$24.95
1439	Collector's Encyclopedia of **Flow Blue China**, Gaston	$19.95
3812	Collector's Encyclopedia of **Flow Blue China**, 2nd Ed., Gaston	$24.95
3813	Collector's Encyclopedia of **Hall China**, 2nd Ed., Whitmyer	$24.95
3431	Collector's Encyclopedia of **Homer Laughlin China**, Jasper	$24.95
1276	Collector's Encyclopedia of **Hull Pottery**, Roberts	$19.95
4573	Collector's Encyclopedia of **Knowles, Taylor & Knowles**, Gaston	$24.95
3962	Collector's Encyclopedia of **Lefton China**, DeLozier	$19.95
2210	Collector's Encyclopedia of **Limoges Porcelain**, 2nd Ed., Gaston	$24.95
2334	Collector's Encyclopedia of **Majolica Pottery**, Katz-Marks	$19.95
1358	Collector's Encyclopedia of **McCoy Pottery**, Huxford	$19.95
3963	Collector's Encyclopedia of **Mctlox Potteries**, Gibbs Jr.	$24.95
3313	Collector's Encyclopedia of **Niloak**, Gifford	$19.95
3837	Collector's Encyclopedia of **Nippon Porcelain I**, Van Patten	$24.95
2089	Collector's Ency. of **Nippon Porcelain**, 2nd Series, Van Patten	$24.95
1665	Collector's Ency. of **Nippon Porcelain**, 3rd Series, Van Patten	$24.95
3836	**Nippon Porcelain** Price Guide, Van Patten	$9.95
1447	Collector's Encyclopedia of **Noritake**, Van Patten	$19.95
3432	Collector's Encyclopedia of **Noritake**, 2nd Series, Van Patten	$24.95
1037	Collector's Encyclopedia of **Occupied Japan**, Vol. I, Florence	$14.95
1038	Collector's Encyclopedia of **Occupied Japan**, Vol. II, Florence	$14.95
2088	Collector's Encyclopedia of **Occupied Japan**, Vol. III, Florence	$14.95
2019	Collector's Encyclopedia of **Occupied Japan**, Vol. IV, Florence	$14.95
2335	Collector's Encyclopedia of **Occupied Japan**, Vol. V, Florence	$14.95
3964	Collector's Encyclopedia of **Pickard China**, Reed	$24.95
1311	Collector's Encyclopedia of **R.S. Prussia**, 1st Series, Gaston	$24.95
1715	Collector's Encyclopedia of **R.S. Prussia**, 2nd Series, Gaston	$24.95
3726	Collector's Encyclopedia of **R.S. Prussia**, 3rd Series, Gaston	$24.95
3877	Collector's Encyclopedia of **R.S. Prussia**, 4th Series, Gaston	$24.95
1034	Collector's Encyclopedia of **Roseville Pottery**, Huxford	$19.95
1035	Collector's Encyclopedia of **Roseville Pottery**, 2nd Ed., Huxford	$19.95
3357	**Roseville** Price Guide No. 10	$9.95
2083	Collector's Encyclopedia of **Russel Wright** Designs, Kerr	$19.95
3965	Collector's Encyclopedia of **Sascha Brastoff**, Conti, Bethany & Seay	$24.95

OTHER COLLECTIBLES

2269	Antique **Brass & Copper** Collectibles, Gaston	$16.95
1880	Antique **Iron**, McNerney	$9.95
3872	Antique **Tins**, Dodge	$24.95
1714	**Black** Collectibles, Gibbs	$19.95
1128	**Bottle** Pricing Guide, 3rd Ed., Cleveland	$7.95
3959	**Cereal Box** Bonanza, The 1950's, Bruce	$19.95
3718	Collectible **Aluminum**, Grist	$16.95
3445	Collectible **Cats**, An Identification & Value Guide, Fyke	$18.95
4560	Collectible **Cats**, An Identification & Value Guide, Book II, Fyke	$19.95
4563	Collector's Encyclopedia of **Wall Pockets**, Newbound	$19.95
1634	Collector's Ency. of Figural & Novelty **Salt & Pepper Shakers**, Davern	$19.95
2020	Collector's Ency. of Figural & Novelty **Salt & Pepper Shakers**, Vol. II, Davern	$19.95
2018	Collector's Encyclopedia of **Granite Ware**, Greguire	$24.95
3430	Collector's Encyclopedia of **Granite Ware**, Book II, Greguire	$24.95
3879	Collector's Guide to **Antique Radios**, 3rd Ed., Bunis	$18.95
1916	Collector's Guide to **Art Deco**, Gaston	$14.95
3880	Collector's Guide to **Cigarette Lighters**, Flanagan	$17.95
1537	Collector's Guide to **Country Baskets**, Raycraft	$9.95
3966	Collector's Guide to **Inkwells**, Identification & Values, Badders	$18.95
3881	Collector's Guide to **Novelty Radios**, Bunis/Breed	$18.95
3729	Collector's Guide to **Snow Domes**, Guarnaccia	$18.95
3730	Collector's Guide to **Transistor Radios**, Bunis	$15.95
2276	**Decoys**, Kangas	$24.95
1629	**Doorstops**, Identification & Values, Bertoia	$9.95
4567	Figural **Napkin Rings**, Gottschalk & Whitson	$18.95
3968	**Fishing Lure** Collectibles, Murphy/Edmisten	$24.95
3817	**Flea Market Trader**, 10th Ed., Huxford	$12.95
3976	Foremost Guide to **Uncle Sam** Collectibles, Czulewicz	$24.95
3819	**General Store Collectibles**, Wilson	$24.95
2215	Goldstein's **Coca-Cola** Collectibles	$16.95
3884	Huxford's Collectible **Advertising**, 2nd Ed.	$24.95
2216	**Kitchen Antiques**, 1790–1940, McNerney	$14.95
3321	Ornamental & Figural **Nutcrackers**, Rittenhouse	$16.95
2026	**Railroad** Collectibles, 4th Ed., Baker	$14.95
1632	**Salt & Pepper Shakers**, Guarnaccia	$9.95
1888	**Salt & Pepper Shakers** II, Identification & Value Guide, Book II, Guarnaccia	$14.95
2220	**Salt & Pepper Shakers** III, Guarnaccia	$14.95
3443	**Salt & Pepper Shakers** IV, Guarnaccia	$18.95
4555	**Schroeder's Antiques Price Guide**, 14th Ed., Huxford	$14.95
2096	**Silverplated Flatware**, Revised 4th Edition, Hagan	$14.95
1922	Standard **Old Bottle** Price Guide, Sellari	$14.95
3892	**Toy & Miniature Sewing Machines**, Thomas	$18.95
3828	Value Guide to **Advertising Memorabilia**, Summers	$18.95
3977	Value Guide to **Gas Station** Memorabilia, Summers & Priddy	$24.95
4572	**Wall Pockets** of the Past, Perkins	$17.95
3444	**Wanted to Buy**, 5th Edition	$9.95